Gypsy Wedding Dreams

THELMA MADINE

Gypsy Wedding Dreams

10 DRESSES. 10 DREAMS.
All the secrets revealed.

THELMA MADINE

Harper
Collins

HarperCollins*Publishers*
77–85 Fulham Palace Road,
Hammersmith, London W6 8JB

www.harpercollins.co.uk

First published by HarperCollins*Publishers* 2013

10 9 8 7 6 5 4 3 2 1

Photographs: pp14, 80, 102, 123, 125, 232, 233,
235 and 237 courtesy of Firecracker Films. All other
photography courtesy of the author.

A catalogue record of this book is available from the
British Library

ISBN   978-0-00-745698-7

Prepress and colour origination by Group FMG.
Printed and bound in China by RR Donnelley

To all the beautiful brides
we've ever worked with.

Contents

Introduction

I have enjoyed working with the traveller community ever since they first started coming to me, 20 years ago, when I worked on a market stall in Liverpool. I've made some wonderful friends among them, and throughout my career, I've felt their support and warmth.

I've done proms, First Communions, engagement parties, all sorts … But of course the one area that has had the biggest impact – on both my business and my personal life – is the weddings. It's through preparing for these big days with the girls that I've got to know both them and their way of life better than when I'm putting together any other type of creation. Because gypsy weddings are not like non-traveller weddings, from the intricate specifics of their customs and traditions to the unbelievable imagination and determination that they put into getting the wedding dresses and outfits that will bring their dreams to life. Each time I take an order for a new wedding, I am not just accepting a new piece of business: I am beginning a new journey.

But some of those journeys have been bumpy rides, to say the least! Along the way there have been tears, tantrums and tiaras. I've seen girls threaten to cut all their hair off if they don't get their own way and I've had them pleading and begging with me to keep their darkest secrets. And I've seen families reach the brink of collapse through bitter feuding about the tiniest details and exchanged the level of kindness with them that I would normally reserve for my own family. Yet despite all the dramas and the heartache that I've seen along the way, there isn't a single experience that I would take back; each and every wedding has been a mini saga of its own, and I've loved them all.

The stories included here are my Top Ten most memorable weddings. They're not all about the dress, although there are dresses here that have changed the course of my career and my dressmaking business, Nico, forever.

And they're not just about the wedding day itself either; after all, for many of these brides, it's the journey to the altar – and all of the negotiating and heartache that this can involve – that is the biggest part of the picture. But every single one of these ten weddings has been something really special to me. They're a real window into the worlds of both Nico and all its chaotic splendour and the travelling community and its secretive ways. Whether you laugh, cry or simply enjoy the gorgeous dresses, I hope you get as much fun out of these ten most extraordinary gypsy weddings as I have.

To the happy couples!

CHAPTER ONE

Inspirations

Joleen

It's a gorgeous gown, with folded petals around the bodice and big swooping skirts – a real fantasy look. But there was one girl who wanted her entire wedding to look like the movie, and that was Joleen Quinn.

As a dressmaker, it's my job to know which are the biggest trends in the fashion industry. I think everyone knows that the one dress that has had the biggest impact on popular culture in recent times is the Sarah Burton for Alexander McQueen dress designed for Kate Middleton's marriage to Prince William on 29 April 2011. And yet the one dress that I have never, ever been asked to copy for a traveller wedding is that very same dress.

They might not always dress to your taste or mine, but there is no denying that the traveller community have their own sense of style and it's completely uninfluenced by what might be driving looks on the high street or in high fashion. It's incredible, really. These days you can hardly open a magazine without finding an image and an accompanying article telling you what a style icon Kate Middleton is, but the gypsy community has been left entirely untouched by her taste, despite several of them coming to me every week and telling me that they want to look like a princess. Yes, the traveller girls dream of being a princess for a day, but they definitely do not wish to be a princess in nude patent leather courts! Really, it's hard not to admire this when you see a million others copying Kate's style, but what always fascinates me is what does actually influence them. Travellers don't go to clubs like other girls, they don't see the same websites; they don't really read fashion magazines, preferring the fantasy worlds of colouring books and dolls. And some of them cannot read so they are totally unaffected by advertising or fashion talk in magazines. Not one of them has ever come in and asked me to make them look like a pop star – we have had the odd Lady Gaga-influenced request but never anyone wanting to look like Katy Perry or one of The Saturdays. Instead they see shapes and colours that they like, and that's what leads them to make the decisions for their special day.

As time passes, and I've seen more and more brides come through the doors at Nico, I have come to realise that what

Inspirations: Joleen

14

Inspirations: Joleen

these girls are looking for is not a dress but a costume. They don't want to look like the most beautiful version of themselves on their wedding day, they want to look like someone else entirely. Nothing should reflect their normal day-to-day lives or chime in with any sense of style that they might usually stick to; they want to take on a different personality entirely, to be something 'other' than usual, not 'better'.

Sometimes the girls want to use brands that they associate with wealth, such as Swarovski, Christian Dior or Baby Phat, but sometimes it's just brands with logos that the girls like. In the past we have been asked to incorporate brand names or logos onto the wedding dresses themselves, but we always try and change them a little so as not to infringe copyright. I don't think the travellers really want to persuade people that those are the brands they're wearing; they just want to make the point that it's where their taste lies. One of our biggest requests is for the exotic pink wedding dress from the 1980s Eddie Murphy film, *Coming to America*. It might seem like a bizarre reference but if you look closely, that dress, with its gold headdress and huge pink swagged skirts, is something truly spectacular. I have made ones like that for weddings, proms and First Communions – it's an all-time favourite.

One of the other inspirational superstars as far as these girls are concerned is Barbie – but not just any old Barbie, really specific ones. Where non-traveller girls might idolise 'Safari Barbie' or 'Swimming Barbie' – you know, the Barbies who actually do something – the traveller girls focus on two classics: 'Bridal Barbie' and 'Barbie of Swan Lake'.

Inspirations: Joleen

Neither does much beyond looking pretty and they don't come with any kit or accessories, unlike some of the more action-focused ones, but both wear really traditional, floaty ballgown-type dresses.

The traveller girls play with Barbies a lot when they're little and they also spend a lot of time drawing them, even when they get a bit older. When small cousins and sisters come into Nico with their older relatives – perhaps if they're going to be bridesmaids or even a mini-bride (see Chapter 3) – they always seem to have colouring books with them, and often they're Barbie ones.

Now we all know that Barbie's proportions are not normal, they're cartoonish, but it's that extreme femininity that the travellers go for – a tiny waist with the corset pulled in as tightly as possible, boobs as high as they can go and huge hips created by my now-famous skirts are the order of the day. These days, I almost don't trust a traveller girl if she says she just wants a slim-fitting skirt!

I am frequently surprised to see that some of these girls don't have automatically pointed feet just like Barbie when

I've finished getting them ready for their big day.

Perhaps as a result of all this colouring-in, I often get really creative designs sent to me from the brides-to-be. It's not unusual for them to have been keeping a little scrapbook of images for years, so when they come to place an order for their wedding dress they will bring in their own sketches of how they want it to look, complete with directions on what fabrics they want to use or how the skirts should hang.

I love seeing those images as they give me an idea of what is driving the girl's dreams, who she really wants to be on the day and how I can help her to be that person. Sometimes I can even work out where a bride's priorities lie just by looking at how firmly the pen has been pressed into the pad in different areas on the page – there's nothing like direct access to a customer's original idea to help create the perfect dress.

17

Inspirations: Joleen

But there's one brand name that influences designs even more than good old Barbie: Disney. Every time there's a new Disney heroine out in the cinema, I make it my business to check what she looks like as I know I'll be making versions of her gown for the next couple of years. Since my own little girl Katrina was born eight years ago, I often find myself taking her to the cinema for a 'treat' only to head down there with a sketchpad and pencil, keen to see what the lines on the dresses are.

After one Disney film came out Katrina was given a Disney doll, but I stole it to keep in the office for showing brides. It was too good to resist, and has proved every bit as useful as I'd hoped in helping to explain ideas to traveller girls!

The most recent Disney production to make a big impact was *The Princess and the Frog* (2009). That film led to us making one of our most memorable wedding outfits ever. Everyone wanted 'Princess and the Frog' dresses that year. From the month the film was released I was inundated with images printed off the Internet of the now-familiar green-and-pastel-toned dress. It's a gorgeous gown, with folded petals around the bodice and big swooping skirts – a real fantasy look. But there was one traveller girl who wanted her entire wedding to look just like the movie, and that was Joleen Quinn.

Joleen first came to see me just before the film was released. It was before *My Big Fat Gypsy Wedding* had aired so the shop was much quieter than it is now and she just walked in and got an appointment there and then. She was a lovely girl – very dark, with striking features and gorgeous big green eyes. I immediately warmed to her as she seemed to have a lot on her plate, with lots of younger brothers and sisters around her that she was keeping an eye on. Despite this she had a real air of calm about her; she was lovely and mild-mannered.

'Your time will come soon,' I remember her saying to one of her little sisters, who was watching everything with great big saucer eyes, transfixed by all we did. Visibly excited, she grinned back. I imagine her own scrapbook of ideas is filling up nicely now.

That first time, Joleen was stuck on a Spanish theme for her wedding. She ordered a pink Flamenco-style dress with a very tight-fitting bodice and a huge train. Full of ruffles and Latin detail, it would have been extremely dramatic.

The plan was for a 22-foot train with 40 3D sparkling lilies cascading down the back of it. She was to be accompanied by eight bridesmaids and four page boys between the ages of six and two. And her mum was to have a dress made by Nico as well. Everyone in the bridal party would match the Spanish theme to spectacular effect. This was a big order and they were going all out.

What usually happens after this initial meeting is that we draw up sketches of what was discussed with us in person. These are a combination of the girl's original plans and our input regarding what's technically possible as well as any other ideas that may have come up when the customer became inspired by the atmosphere and details in the factory. Leanne is great at these sketches. Not only can she draw what seem like incredibly intricate dress designs at the bat of an eyelid, she also has a wonderful eye for detail too, making the girls in the sketches have gorgeous floaty hair and dramatic sweeping eyelashes. We send these to the bride-to-be and her family then wait to hear back about any amendments that need to be made to accommodate either their taste or budget. After this comes the request for the deposit to make sure they're really serious. Then, a month or two before the wedding, we start making the gown.

At the beginning of every week we have a meeting to discuss what we'll be working on next in the factory. Sometimes we come across a folder for a girl that we haven't heard from in a while, or maybe a girl for whose gown we haven't even had a deposit. That's when the queries begin.

Inspirations: Joleen

Such was the case with Joleen. When it came to looking at her file again, we realised that we had not heard from her in a long time. It's not that unusual for a girl to go quiet for a while – after all, these people lead lives dictated by travel – but this seemed odd. She had first come in to see us in October with a view to her wedding being the following March. Now it was January and we needed to know whether to get going with Joleen's dress or to abandon the plans; we were just at the point of abandoning hope of ever hearing from the girl again.

To be honest, I had given up on her and was really only humouring the team on it. As far as I was concerned, either this girl had gone with another designer or love's path had not run smoothly for her.

Without telling Leanne or her mother Pauline (who is also my ever-trusted manager at Nico), I took the folder out and put it to one side. After all, it had been a year.

I didn't throw it away, though, as we always keep the files. Some girls have different reasons for not wanting to marry: the groom gets locked up, family finances fluctuate, travelling gets in the way. They are, after all, travellers. In the meantime the latest Disney film had come out, but none of us had seen it. I'd been promising Katrina but we'd not made it yet.

Then, one sunny January morning, Joleen and her family appeared in the shop again. It was as if nothing unusual had happened at all. There was very little explanation as to where she had been but that's sometimes how these things go so I just went along with it.

'It's all changed, Thelma,' she told me with a smile.

'Oh right, has it now?' I replied. 'I suppose you want something really fancy this time' was what I wanted to say but I bit my tongue instead.

'I've seen the new Disney,' she explained, 'and now I want a *Princess and the Frog* theme.'

'OK,' I replied. 'We can do that – of course we can, love. Let's get Leanne and her sketchpad, shall we?'

'Is that OK, Thelma? Is it really?' she excitedly asked.

'It's fine, it's up to you,' I replied. 'You can have it if you want.'

It really wasn't a big deal for us – we are used to dealing with a bit of change and I know things are often unpredictable, so I took a deep breath: it was going to be a long day. They had brought a lot of children with them, who looked as if they had plenty of noisy toys that they were looking forward to playing with. At this point Joleen pulled a whole load of colouring books out of her bag and started to show me pictures of the Disney images that she wanted her dress to look like. There were stickers on one side of the page and line drawings ready to be coloured in on the other; key images had been printed off the Internet and stuck around the pages of the colouring book too.

I couldn't have been more right about that day being long. They talked and talked, going over the new plans again and again. In fact, the young kids made so much noise and distraction that not long after that visit we began to tell people that they couldn't bring small children with them as we don't insure for them to be in there with the machines whirring and bolts of fabric everywhere. It just started to make me uneasy, the number of kids we'd sometimes have running about – I didn't want anyone hurting themselves because I hadn't spoken up.

Now the wedding dress had changed from pink to white. The skirts and the shape of the dress had changed too – very *Princess and the Frog*. And different types of diamanté were being brought up. It was all getting a bit out of hand. I got the feeling that the girl needed a few firm boundaries if colours and dates were starting to change this much.

'Listen, love,' I said. 'All of this is fine, but you've not paid anything beyond the deposit yet and there's a lot of change happening here.'

I looked at her mum. 'You're going to have to reassure me that these really are the plans now. We're not going to be able to actually start making this dress until you pay a bit more of the fee.'

'No problem,' said the mum, straight away. She seemed very relaxed about everything – in some ways, a little bit too relaxed.

She was an absolutely beautiful woman – she could have been a model, she was so statuesque – and she had a real natural beauty. But she did not seem especially bothered by her role as a mum. It wasn't the first time I'd seen such a set-up but this particular mum was almost slightly off-hand about the kids, leaving it largely to Joleen to keep an eye on them. It was as if she'd done her years of hard graft, she still looked good and she wanted to enjoy herself and her moment of looking fabulous as the mother-of-the-bride.

You've got to remember these women are not 'mothers-of-the-bride' in the traditional way that we would recognise them – they are women in their mid-thirties, who have married and had kids very young. They've put in a couple of decades of hard graft and now they're sitting back for the party season.

While we sat there in the factory, Joleen was running round keeping an eye on the kids while Mrs Quinn worked through a selection of no fewer than four potential mother-of-the-bride dresses with me. Initially she had planned something very Spanish, with an almost entirely see-through corset to match Joleen's original Latin theme. That dress would have been very elaborate and highly coloured in parts. Then there was talk – for some time – of an ivory dress. It seemed she had a kind of tribute bridal dress in mind. I raised my eyebrows, a little, but went with it. After this there were more changes and then she struck on her final idea.

At the time there were a couple of magazines in the factory that one of the girls had been flicking through during her lunch break. In one of them there was an article featuring a selection of celebrity wedding dresses, including Cheryl Cole's gown from her wedding to Ashley. Straight away, this particular dress caught Mrs Quinn's eye.

'Ooh, now I'd love something like that!' she exclaimed.

'OK,' I replied.

'It's gorgeous, isn't it? And she's such a stunner!'

'Yeah, it's a great dress,' I agreed. I had always liked that dress – it was glamorous without being too flamboyant.

'Which bit of the dress do you think you'd like to be the inspiration?' I asked, wondering if it would be the fitted skirt, the wide train at the back, the way that the skirt kicked out

Inspirations: Joleen

at the bottom or the strapless corseted bodice with trails of sequins working their way down from the waist across the fabric.

'The dress,' she said.
'I'm not sure what you mean, love.'
'I'd like my dress to look like that one,' she said, her face totally deadpan.
'What – the whole dress? You just want a copy?'
'Yes please, love.'

And sure enough, she did. She wasn't interested in being inspired by the new Mrs Cole, she wanted an actual replica. I'm not sure how I would have felt if my mum had turned up on my big day dressed as one of the most famous pop stars in the country, but things are different in the traveller community, and this mum was determined to look her absolute best. And there seemed no lack of love between the two of them. We promised to do as good a version as we could for Mrs Quinn before turning our attention back to Joleen, who had been happily minding the kids for all of this time.

By the end of that day, plans for the new version of the wedding dress were shaping up to be spectacular. It was to have more diamanté on it than any other dress I had done at that stage. There was a lily pad 3D flower – sitting just off

Inspirations: Joleen

her hip, where the corset met the skirt – to further reflect the 'Princess and the Frog' theme, and then there were curling leaves coming down the skirt from the waist. Initially these leaves were to be edged in diamonds but soon plans were in place for them to be entirely filled in with crystals. The flowers were to be 3D, as were the tendrils flowing down her body, so that they were filled out and curling in different directions, standing out from the bodice and skirt. The colours were now white and silver, with huge diamanté sections. Sparkles would be provided by the Swarovski 'Aurora borealis' – the most expensive type of gem we use. These special crystals display different colours depending on the light and the way you look at them. They have to be ordered from Swarovski or a Swarovski agent.

It was going to be a real statement wedding. But then came the biggest statement of all …
'And then for the Frog Prince outfit–' Joleen began.
'OK,' I said, wondering where on earth this was going. Could I even make a 'Frog Prince' suit?
'I'd like my fiancé in it,' she said.

I nodded slowly, desperate to take her seriously but equally sure that no traveller man would ever go along with this. There's no way I'm even going to cut out the fabric for this idea, I thought to myself.

'He's a big fat ugly thing,' interjected the mum. 'A suit like that would be wasted on him!'
It was hard not to laugh.
'But he's my Frog Prince!' protested Joleen.
'Are you sure he'll wear it, love?' I asked delicately.

After all, the suit in question comprised a little cape, silver sequined epaulettes on the shoulders and an old-fashioned high collar with three diamanté fastenings down the front of the pseudo-medieval jacket. As for the trousers, they were a sort of bloomers. Both the jacket and trousers had ruffles on the cuffs. It reminded me a lot of the kids' clothes I used to make on my old market stall but it was not, one might say, the most masculine of outfits for the modern man.

But Joleen seemed sure about it, so I had a look at some more pictures with her and made notes. I was wondering how the hell I was going to make anything wearable out of the situation but I knew I had to make her dreams come true.

Not long afterwards, Joleen called Nico.

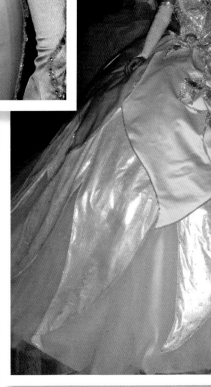

'He isn't going to wear it …' she began.

I could not say I was surprised.

'… But I still want the suit there at the wedding, to complete the theme.'

'OK, love – but how are you going to do that?' I asked.

'I want you to make it for my little brother,' she explained. 'He's a page boy and he'll be there with me, so he can be my Frog Prince.'

'Well, I suppose that outfit is a little kinder to a small boy than it is to a grown man,' I said, relieved to know I wouldn't be making something that would never be worn after all. Joleen was really determined to have all of her Disney characters at that wedding, no matter how bizarre it might have seemed. And I have to say, it's still one of the most memorable weddings I've ever made outfits for.

When they sent through the pictures of the wedding day itself we gathered round and cooed at how fabulous they had all looked – even though the groom was just wearing a standard morning suit. Joleen's little brother looked gorgeous in his Frog Prince suit – a real cutie – and her mum was as statuesque and sexy as we'd anticipated, a real archetype of a woman.

Joleen herself was glowing, thrilled to have got her theme together just as she had imagined. She was absolutely delighted with the results we got for her and couldn't thank us enough.

After that wedding we took loads of orders for similar designs, both for weddings and First Communions. We've done about 50 of them now, and that's just in a couple of years. The First Communion dresses in particular are adorable in that design – the young girls look so cute and they're so influenced by the bigger brides; they're always thrilled when they're allowed this.

Seeing Joleen plan that wedding, and the way that her relationship with her mother and her siblings worked, really helped me to understand why these brides choose the dresses that they do.

Yes, the community is very small so they have to fight harder to stand out in the competition for a good husband, but it's more than that. Very often these girls – who are still only in their teens – have already been looking after younger siblings for years, having left school at around 11. Joleen's life at that point was a really hard graft. She had already been a mother for years, and I could see why becoming a wife so young seemed like an attractive option: she wanted a break. Then the cycle begins again: the girls get married, have children of their own and work hard until the younger ones can start taking over again. By the time they're 40, it's back to living it up again.

But these girls have so much to do at home when they are in their mid- to late teens that the idea of being a princess for a day is all-consuming.

It's what they've dreamt of while they've been cleaning and feeding the kids and doing whatever else needs to be done. They're living adult lives but with little idea of what kind of adult they're going to be.

This process of trying on dresses and chopping and changing back and forth between princesses and fairies and ballerinas and Barbies is not just to do with the look on the day, but with trying on different personalities.

Inspirations: Joleen

It's a case of 'Which me do I want to be on this day?', 'Who says most about my dreams and the woman I want to become?'

Often the dresses they choose are not based on real women but blank slates with no real story behind them, precisely because it gives them a bit of space to imagine their future selves.

They don't have the chance to find themselves a career, go travelling and try out a few boyfriends before deciding what kind of a woman they plan to be – they do it while choosing their dress, which is why I always do my very best to be patient and respectful during the process, even if some of the ideas do seem a little unusual at first.

Inspirations: Joleen

CHAPTER TWO

The Cryer

Ashleigh

My blood went cold and I completely froze as I realised who I was talking to. That girl, the one we had sworn we would never work with again.

I've got very little to complain about at Nico, but every now and again we have a bride in who really pushes us to the limit. Lateness, disorganisation, even chaos with the finances … these, I can deal with. But some girls really are a nightmare. And for them, we have 'The Book'. There is no actual book – it's more of a list that we keep in the office that has on it the names of people we will never work with again: the ones who simply aren't worth the trouble, those who have been unforgivably rude or simply wasted too much of our time.

The Cryer: Ashleigh

Ashleigh Monaghan is the best example of this, as well as being the exception. Because despite her being in The Book, we still ended up making her wedding dress. It all began with her engagement dress, which we did not meet her for. Flamingo pink, it was for a July engagement. It came in two pieces: a halterneck, with leaves all the way around her neck and collar, and then a short skirt with a long train at the back. She had 3D roses all over it – wired up so that they didn't sit flat on the dress but stood out to make a stunning dramatic statement.

But she was pressure: every day was pressure. Ashleigh wanted more and more from us, and we'd give her more, but then she didn't want to pay for it. She would snap at her mum, she would shout at us if she didn't like our answer and then she would be on the phone at all times of day and night. I had Ashleigh and her mum on the phone, both pleading from different angles sometimes. Even though we never met her then, she still made it into The Book. Not formally, but we had marked her as difficult from the very beginning.

That engagement dress was an absolute stunner. We had girls come into the factory while it was being made or before it was sent off to her and they actually cried when they saw it. Honestly, they were that sad it wasn't their dress, their idea, that they burst into tears. I'd never had that before and I was glad that at least someone was getting pleasure out of the dress because by that stage Pauline had started to take all the phone calls in the factory, lying that I was either out or busy – I couldn't take any more. Over the years she has got pretty

41

good at those fake calls – 'She's just popped to the bank, love, sorry!', 'She's on a trip for a wedding, love, sorry!' – and so on. But she had never had to handle them in such volume before. When she finally got it, apparently Ashleigh did love the dress; she called me, crying on the phone because she loved it so much. She was very over-emotional, in as positive a way now as she had been with her negativity before. I was thrilled that she loved it, but after I put the phone down on that call I said to the rest of the team:

'Well, we just have to make sure we don't do her wedding! If she behaves like that over an engagement dress, we'll never hear the end of the wedding.'

There had been talk of a wedding dress while we were negotiating the engagement dress. She wanted us to do it – sometimes people say they are going to use us for their wedding dress so they can get some gloves or a couple of extras thrown in on the engagement dress – but she was quite sure that she wanted to use me. But this time I stayed quiet; I just kept my mouth shut whenever there was talk of 'the next dress', for my sake and the rest of the team.

Some months later we received the measurements and a drawing for a wedding dress order through the mail. This wasn't entirely unusual because sometimes travellers are literally travelling while they're planning a wedding and can't make it to the shop for a first fitting. If they're very sure of their size – either because they've had one of my dresses before as a bridesmaid or for a party, or because they've been fitted in the past – and their dream design, often they just trust me with the rest. In with the usual selection of crank mail and bizarre charity requests, we'll get a scrap of handwritten paper that is in fact an entirely serious order. If I've worked with a bride that the family might know and they've seen that I get it done how and when I've said I will, they don't worry as much about meeting me.

Often I'll get the design – sometimes just a basic drawing and lots of description – along with the measurements, and we'll get back to them with our finished suggested design, this time drawn up properly by Leanne or me, and a quote. It's pretty simple once you've done it a few times, and it can save a lot of time and drama with some brides!

The Cryer: Ashleigh

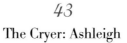

In this case, the order – together with an initial sketch of the design – came from a woman whose name we had not heard before, but she seemed very organised and familiar with the process, so none of us thought to question it. There was no need to make a fuss where one wasn't needed, we thought.

The inspiration was *Barbie of Swan Lake*, with diaphanous fairy wings on the upper arms and a similar design flowing down over the large underskirts beneath; it all looked very delicate, very floaty. We sent back our drawings and an estimate of the cost. At this point there were no names mentioned, apart from that on the envelope.

The deposit arrived straight away, with no problems at all. A few weeks later I was chatting to the mother, confirming price details of some alterations we were making to add to the dress, when she said: 'That's the thing – the engagement dress was so spectacular that we all feel under pressure to make this one even better. It has to top the engagement dress, and that's no mean feat.'

'Really, love, who did the engagement dress then?' I asked, confused why she was putting me under so much pressure.
'You did, Thelma,' came the reply.

My blood went cold and I completely froze as I realised who I was talking to. There was no question about it. It was that girl – the one we had sworn we would never work with again.

Once the conversation had ended I turned back to the rest of the team, my head in my hands.

'How the hell have we taken this order?' I asked.

The girls said it couldn't be her, but I knew it was. We all sat round and tried to work it out.

'It can't be her,' said Leanne. 'It's not her name on the order.'

'It's her,' I said. I was annoyed, we were in too deep: she had paid her deposit and it was a dress we knew we could do a good job with. We had to do the dress. How had we not known it was her?

It was only later that I spotted in the files that the mother had used *her* name to place the wedding dress order rather than use Ashleigh's name, which would have been usual. None of us had remembered the mum's name from the engagement order as she was very mild mannered, and so many travellers have the same surname that we really only refer to brides by their first name and the design of the dress – for example, 'Cherry girl' or 'Shell girl'. That's all we write on the files until we've got to know the bride and her family a bit better.

46

The Cryer: Ashleigh

We really would have said a flat-out no, had we had realised it was Ashleigh. Not because we disliked her but because she was so relentless. But we'd made an agreement, and we'd taken the money, so before long we were busy making the dress. And, as I'd feared, we were quickly doing five times more work for that one gown than for any other customer. The phone calls, the negotiations, the questions, it felt all-consuming, and it made me protective of the rest of our customers – it wasn't fair that their experience was being infringed upon because of one girl making a huge fuss. Even bearing in mind the years I have spent dealing with the traveller community and all their quirks, this was way

beyond anything we could cope with at Nico. It wasn't a tradition I didn't understand, it was pure mayhem.

Part of the reason why it became such a huge saga was that Ashleigh wouldn't talk to me directly. She would call – several times a day – but put her mother on the phone while she was in the background, yelling. I could have had a straight conversation with her and got it out of her what she wanted a bit faster, but that wasn't how Ashleigh wanted to do things. So I had to deal with her mother trying to 'translate' what she wanted. It was never, ever a simple conversation.

They'd always start in the same way: 'Ooh, Thelma,' her mother's now-familiar soft voice would say, 'What she'd like is this, love.'

I would start to reply when I'd hear her shouting in the background; she thought we didn't understand her, we were trying to make her unhappy, we were ganging up on her.

All the while she kept adding things onto the dress. The mum would phone up and say, 'She wants these 3D Hawaiian flowers on here, here and here.' It was as if Ashleigh would go to a wedding, see someone with something on their dress and then she would decide she wanted to have a bit of that on her dress too. Every time she went to another wedding, she'd want to add something from it as well. She wanted to outdo all of the other girls' dresses by having something of theirs on her dress.

She went to one wedding we did a dress for – a beautiful-looking kid, a completely different dress to anything we've done before – and first thing in the morning she was barking instructions down the phone.

'She's seen Melissa's dress,' her mum said. 'It was out of this world, outstanding, so handsome. Is our dress going to be better than that?'

'Well, she paid more than you,' was my answer. I was at the end of my tether – I take pride in my work and the work of the team here. We really didn't like being doubted so it was as much as I could offer.

Having said that, Mrs Monaghan was always charming to me, no matter how Ashleigh was behaving in the background. She would always ask how I was; despite the demands, she was lovely to deal with.

And Ashleigh herself was a sweetheart – when I got her direct. It was only with going through the parents that things got silly. The first half of every phone call I'd be thinking, she's OK, really, I shouldn't have been so hard on her. But then she'd turn and the pressure would start.

She was just a 17-year-old girl and I was infuriated by how she'd get a rise out of me. At one stage she decided that she would like an extra 29 3D flowers added to her dress. Those flowers use almost an entire bag of crystals each – they are expensive but, more importantly, they are heavy. And she wanted them attached to the most lightweight of the sheer pieces of fabric that she had flowing down the top of the skirts.

Pauline called her and started explaining to her mum that there was no way we could do that for her unless we went seriously over the budget we'd been given and it would also put the delicate fabric at great risk of ripping under their weight. We were sure they'd just rip off – the whole point of that part of the dress was that it looked flyaway, like a fairy's dress, not for holding bloody great crystal flowers on!

'We can have them maybe dotted around other areas on the dress,' she explained, 'but not on the ends of those petals like that – they'll just pull off.'

These flowers were the size of a saucer each; they were a serious amount of extra material and work. As I suspected, later that day Mrs Monaghan called about the costs: 'Oh no, we can't afford it.'

Away went another entire day of extra work we'd spent on the dress and now we were just met with not getting paid for the cancelled work and yet more of Ashleigh's shouting from behind her mother. Each time we'd had one of these conversations it took up the best part of a working morning or afternoon. One minute she wanted a belly top with huge skirts. Usually, if a girl's having a belly top, her skirts are lower on the hip and slim-fitting, creating a bit of a slinky line. And if they're having big skirts, they tend to have a corset which covers where the skirts are fastened. My skirts are so heavy that they really need to sit up on the waist, with the girl's hips for the lower skirts to rest on. So a belly top with big skirts really doesn't work – it'll either sit on the hips and slide down under their own weight, or look a fright up round her waist. But whichever way we tried to explain this to Ashleigh, she still didn't understand why large skirts wouldn't physically hold up on a dress like that; she would not have it.

The next minute there would be another quibble about the underskirts. Then there would be a panic about revised costs. And inevitably there would be more upsets, which often ended with the mother handing the phone over.

53

'Here, you speak to Thelma,' Mrs Monaghan would say to her daughter and then turn back to me: 'It's only you she listens to anyway.'

It had reached the point in the factory where it would get to about 11am – the machines would be whirring, we'd have cups of tea on the go, the banter was good – and someone would always look up and say, 'Has Ash called yet?'

We were all waiting for it, the whole time, because we knew that once she called the mood would change and we'd be running around, trying to sort out the latest drama. It was a horrible tension to be working with by the end.

Sometimes it would be eight or nine o'clock at night and there'd be no one there but me and the phone would still be going. If I didn't pick up it would ring again – and again, and again. It was merciless.

I couldn't just sit there and work on a dress or catch up on paperwork. Oh no! She would carry on leaving messages.

'It's very important, Thelma …'

'It's Ashleigh's mummy here …'

'Thelma, we really do need to talk to you before bed …'

Eventually I would relent and it would be something silly, like, 'Ash is wondering, have you started the flowers yet?'

I liked the woman – she was polite and kind, but a bit of a pushover. One evening when I pointed out that perhaps the fourth query of the day could have waited, she replied, 'Ooh, you know what they're like!'

'Well, I know what yours is like,' I said, 'but if mine spoke to me like that she'd get a smack in the gob.'

I knew this woman didn't have any more money to spend but she so wanted to make her daughter happy and give her a dream day. But Ashleigh wanted constant reassurance; the more she nagged, the more she got.

Girls that call in a lot are not uncommon, and I don't really have a problem with it. I understand what a big deal these dresses are, for the mother and the bride. But there was only one other time we had a girl who rang as much as Ashleigh and she wasn't nearly

as much pressure. Don't get me wrong, the constant chatting was not ideal, but this girl was a real sweetheart. She was from Belfast and we did her engagement dress, and then her wedding dress. She kept changing her mind about the engagement dress as every time she saw something she'd want it added: after many, many extra drawings the finished garment had feathers, diamonds, flowing arms and all sorts. In shocking pink too!

She'd call in for what seemed like days on end and sometimes for no real reason. She never had complaints, she didn't seem too fussed about how the timings were coming along, and the finances were all agreed, but she'd ask for a few details of what we were up to, check on who else was getting dresses done at the time, or anything else she might think of.

At Nico, we're open on a Saturday and often we're there working on a dress on a Sunday too, but it took a while before Leanne realised that she was calling all weekend – from Friday night for almost 48 hours non-stop. It was starting to feel so personal.

Lovely though she was, the situation was stopping us from getting any actual work done. And after what was nearly two years, what with the engagement dress and then the wedding dress, I felt enough was enough.

In the end I had to say to her, 'Love, this is a lot of phone calls – I'm worried that you're not leaving us with enough time for dressmaking while you've been busying yourself with these chats. How can we get on with making this dress if you keep on at us like this?'

The Cryer: Ashleigh

'I just like talking to you, it's so nice keeping in touch,' she said.

'It's great, but we need to get back to the job in hand …'

'Oh sorry, Thelma, love,' she replied. 'It's just that I get my free minutes at the weekend so I like to call round whoever I can and you're on the list.'

When I put the phone down and told the girls why she'd been ringing so much, they couldn't believe it. We nearly died laughing when we realised we'd been being so polite all because this girl had some free minutes on her mobile contract!

The calls calmed down after that, bless her heart, but she was a very different kettle of fish to Ashleigh.

Ashleigh was her parents' eldest, and it was beyond me how she managed to secure this much power over her mother. What we didn't know, until the day she came to collect the dress, was that she had even more power over her dad.

I was pleasantly surprised by how pretty Ashleigh was when she eventually turned up at the factory. She had very dark hair and fine features. When she came in – on time – she had a real sparkle and I thought that finally, everything was going to be OK.

She walked into the room where her dress stood on a mannequin and gasped. There was tension throughout the

57

factory as we all looked at each other, waiting for her reaction. Her hands flew to her mouth and she took a deep breath.

'I love it!' she screeched.
We all smiled and let out a heavy sigh of relief.
'It's like nothing I've ever seen before – oh my God!'

She really was thrilled, and so was I. We left her to it so that she could start getting out of her clothes to try it on, and waited next door. Then, all of a sudden, almighty screams were coming from the room. I ran in, completely panicked by what could have gone wrong.

'What's happened?'

'There should be 29 flowers on here!' she shrieked.

'Yes, love, we had this conversation – a few times. They would have ripped this fairy wing fabric,' I explained, stroking the petals to show what I meant.

She was crying so much that she couldn't actually get any words out. She literally wasn't making sense. I had heard this down the telephone before, but I had never witnessed it in the flesh.

'Ashleigh, love,' I said. 'Look at the dress – go through it from top to bottom – then you tell us specifically what is not right and we can fix it. Start at the top and we'll work down.

Make a list. Right? Every point of the dress! Standing there crying is not going to do you any good. Stand there, take this pen, and work your way down.'

But she was still crying and her mum was just standing there, consoling her. 'Ashleigh, Ashleigh,' she kept repeating. Her dad had his head in his hands.

'Do you want a cup of coffee, love?' I asked the mum, just looking at her.

'Yes please, Thelma,' she replied in the world-weary voice that I'd heard so many times before.

So I went into the kitchen, made her a coffee, put it on the table in front of her and closed the door for her.

'I love the dress so much, Thelma,' she said, sadly. 'I'm really pleased. And I know Ash is too – she's always like this, though.'

We could still hear her sobs in the kitchen. It was as if she had no way of expressing any extreme of emotion other than this. Crying was the only way she knew to get what she wanted. She'd worked herself up into such a state.

The thing is, you have to remember, this was the day Ashleigh had been dreaming of for years. It's the same for all my young traveller brides, so while it's hard to deal with at the time, you have to bear in mind what a big day it is. The trying-on day is when all their dreams are realised – it is their princess moment. But poor Ashleigh was out of control.

Pauline was in the other room trying to deal with it, trying to persuade her to at least try the dress on and see what it looked like on her. She got out the book with the sketch in it and showed Ashleigh that we had done exactly as we were asked. We were at a loss as to how or where we had gone wrong.

'I know, I know! But it hasn't got this on, or these flowers!' she belted out. Her hands were flailing about, pointing at vague areas where she knew that we had not really made any mistakes.

'But your mum's only got a certain amount of money, love,' I heard Pauline say, trying to placate her. I felt that I must step in at this point: 'Apart from it looking ridiculous if we'd added all the extras you wanted, your mum only has a certain amount that she can pay for,' I told her.

'I won't wear it like that, I won't wear it like that!' she kept saying.

'You've already got nine flowers on there for nothing, love – we just did it to try and keep you happy.'

This was true. Despite my instincts, I had actually given her a huge amount of free work and detail, just to try and make everyone's lives easier. I left her with her pen and paper, trying to make the list of specific problems. Her mum was at the kitchen table, staring down at her mug.

'I could do with you on the day of the wedding,' she told me, 'just to calm her down.'

A little while later Ash came to the door of the kitchen and her face was completely streaked in black from her make-up running, where she'd been crying. Pauline had failed to persuade her to try the dress on so she could see how great it was. So we tried to get her to wipe her face and go and enjoy her moment but we were met with more tears.

'You know me! You know me …'

And then the crying began in earnest. Ashleigh got up and ran out into the street, where her dad was waiting in the car.

Five minutes later, Marta – one of the girls from the factory – came in from having a cigarette.

'That girl is still crying out there,' she told us. 'She's just pacing up and down the road.'

Marta was right, but I don't know whose attention she hoped to get out there because it's a quiet road by some industrial buildings. It's not a fancy area, so I was glad that Pauline's mission to get her into those skirts had failed or she would have been at risk of mucking up her skirts.

She kept going, though. It was like a physical release, like she had to get something out of herself: she was wailing and grabbing at her hair as if she was a mad person in ancient Greece. Even the seagulls were going mad at the noise! It was the kind of crying that always, always gives you a headache when you're the one doing it. How she hadn't worn herself out yet …

I watched her for a bit. In the end it was all of us on the street in silence, just watching her run up and down, pulling at her hair. We must have looked as if we were at Wimbledon: heads turning left, heads turning right …

Just leave her, I said. Let her run up and down – she'll burn it off; she needs to learn to calm herself down. So we went inside and had a cup of coffee.

Eventually we got the dad in and offered him a coffee. He was thrilled to be out of the firing line and before long, Ashleigh had found her way back inside too.

'I've never seen a dress like this in my life,' her dad said, nodding at the mannequin. 'It's something else. But I knew she'd be like this – she's like this wherever we go.'

She was sobbing and stammering, big wracking sobs that went through her whole body.

The drama was non-stop. You've never seen anything like it in all your life. I mean we've had reactions in our time – this place is no stranger to a tantrum. But I have never,

The Cryer: Ashleigh

ever seen a girl react like that – about anything. It was unbelieveable! Especially as she couldn't even specify what was actually upsetting her.

'What is it?' I said for the umpteenth time. 'What is actually wrong?'

It was time for me to put my foot down, as it looked as if no one else was going to. 'Stop screaming or I'm not going to let you have the dress at all – I've had enough! You tell me now: what is it that you want?'

'Well,' she began, her shoulders still juddering. 'Do you think, um, well … What do you think, so what can I do about …?'

Sheepishly she pointed at some areas that she felt weren't up to scratch. She really was pulling at straws now …

'Right! You want some of those flowers filled in. I have told you now that your mum does not have the money for any more.'

'But I want a bigger flower here!' Her bottom lip wobbled.

In the end we agreed to shuffle some stuff around, to create a different, fuller look. We moved flowers to create different effects.

But then when she tried the dress on, the problems started all over again. 'I want it tighter,' she demanded. 'I want it tighter!'

'Well, if you want it even tighter than this then we're going to have to take an inch off each side because the corset is overlapping now.'

The Cryer: Ashleigh

Seconds later she'd be gasping: 'Ooh, I can't breathe! I can't breathe! Why, Thelma, why?'

'You're saying you can't breathe and you want it tighter?'

'Yes, but I still want it tighter.'

'But if you can't breathe now, and you have it tighter, think what it's going to be like then.'

'Oh, I think I'm going to faint – I just can't breathe, I can't breathe!'

In the end, I just said: 'Yes, we'll do that,' just to make her think she'd had it her own way.

It was still another day's work, though, and we'd put a ridiculous amount of effort into that dress already, and we all knew that she'd just been saying things because she needed to justify the fuss that she'd made – there was no other explanation.

The next morning she returned to see the finished dress with its amendments. Every single girl in the company had worked extra to get that dress how she wanted it: extra flowers, taking in the corset, all of it. In this instance crying really did get her what she wanted, despite everything I've always told Katrina, my youngest. I hate to say it, but we just wanted shot of her.

She couldn't hide the smile on her face when she came in, though – she absolutely loved the dress, and we knew it.

When she put it on, she looked a dream and she could not have been more charming – you'd never have known she could be such a terror and she even laughed about her behaviour with us.

The Cryer: Ashleigh

I told her that she'd made such a fuss that I'd put her in this book but she just grinned and looked thrilled that her attention-seeking mission had proved such a success.

But in time, when I had had a bit of a think about the drama, I came to the conclusion that she really wasn't worried about the line of diamonds running across her cleavage that she had mentioned – she was panicking that she was about to lose control over her parents because she was soon to become a married woman. She didn't know if her husband would be as quick to bend to her will, even though her dad told me he was very laid back!

I think that if she'd had those 29 flowers ripping the fabric to shreds as she'd requested, she would still have done the same thing. It was her transition to womanhood that she was crying about, not the dress. She just wanted to keep her mum and dad to hand to keep sorting things out for her, even though on this occasion there wasn't anything to sort out. It was kind of checking, to keep up her skills as best she could.

I never went to that wedding, though. When she left the shop, I leant against the door and slid down it in relief.

A week later I phoned to see how it had gone and she said the wedding wasn't for another month. She had lied about the date to get the dress there with enough extra for a little tantrum time!

CHAPTER THREE

*The Con**

Priscilla

While the mother was in the office sorting out the final payments, I grabbed Leanne and a couple of girls and whispered frantically to them: 'Go into the van right now and grab the boxes with the corsets in them. Go! Go, go, go! Hurry – and then hide them!'

Even when pushed to the limit by drama queens like Ashleigh, I do usually end up being fond of the girls that we work with. They are usually so grateful afterwards, or on the big day itself, that it all seems worth it and I tend to forget about the time I spent tearing my hair out. I like to think that I've got pretty good at working with the traveller community now, that I've seen it all. I know their customs, I understand what's important to them and I admire their sense of style – the way that they're not influenced by fashion in the traditional sense.

The Con: Priscilla

I've even got my head around the way they haggle, not because they always want something for nothing, but because they see it as part of the process – or at least I thought I had. Because there's always the odd exception that proves the rule, and every time I reckon I've learned how not to get into trouble, I find myself having to think again.

One bride's family that really shocked me with their behaviour came about a couple of years ago when we were filming for *My Big Fat Gypsy Wedding*. It was February 2010 and a mum, nan and daughter all came over together to order a lot for the wedding of the bride, a girl named Priscilla. They could not have been more charming, really salt-of-the-earth, friendly people and very easy to deal with that day. They wanted a wedding dress, dresses for five bridesmaids, a best woman, four flower girls and a mini-bride, as well as an outfit for the mother-of-the-bride. It was a big order, but why not? They seemed like a charming, polite family at first. It was all looking nice and straightforward, even by the standards that Nico chaos can sometimes set.

Priscilla herself seemed like a nice girl – she wasn't making a big fuss about things, throwing her weight around and causing trouble; nor was she uncomfortable with the process of deciding what she wanted. She seemed to be quite mature, and handled the decisions and practicalities with a bit of class.

The dress she had chosen was to be an asymmetrical one with a glove for one arm and leaves tumbling down the other. It had a classic Nico bodice with its smooth lines, cinched

The Con: Priscilla

waist, laced back and sparkling embellishments, and huge underskirts and there was a big choker as well.

There was nothing exceptional about it, but she wanted absolutely all of the classic elements included. She wanted huge 3D leaves attached to the skirt, almost as if they were growing out of it – it was very dramatic, and the whole gown was to be covered in diamanté.

At this point in the process there was a bit of debate about whether or not the leaves on the dress were going to be filled in with crystals. It is much less expensive – and less heavy – to have leaves and petal shapes simply edged with the diamanté. The dramatic highlight is created, and the patterns really stand out, but the cost is kept down. It takes way more than double the number of crystals to fill in the shapes – obviously the effect is fabulous but it does significantly add to the weight of the dress, which can be a real consideration for girls with smaller frames.

The compromise that we came to with Priscilla was for the shapes to be double-edged, which has a stronger effect than the single edge but isn't quite so expensive as the full diamanté. But then the order started to grow.

Just when it seemed that the edging decision had been made, the family came back wanting more for the bridesmaids. It's not unusual for the bridesmaids and best woman to be relatively plainly dressed, especially if there is to be a mini-bride, which there was in Priscilla's case. If you have seen the show you will know that a mini-bride is usually a younger relative – a sister or favourite cousin – who is dressed in an exact replica of the bride's outfit. She acts as a sort of assistant throughout the day, while obviously looking adorable.

It's a huge honour for a little girl to be asked to be a mini-bride, as it's not just a sign of being one of the older girl's special relatives, it's also a fantastic opportunity for them to dress up in a really spectacular outfit for the day.

Usually, they're the envy of all their little friends for the period around the wedding. But Priscilla and her mum, Mary, weren't letting plans for the mini-bride get in the way of the bridesmaids' outfits, which started to have amendment after amendment made on them. At first, they began to get a lot of diamonds on their dresses, then there were some butterflies being scattered on them, and then there were gold diamonds rather than the usual bright white that we use.

At this point, around February, *My Big Fat Gypsy Wedding* came on board as they were looking for brides for the show. They were thrilled when they saw the stunning plans that Priscilla had for what was shaping up to be a really fabulous wedding, and while at first Priscilla's mum was a bit sceptical, she ended up being persuaded. Soon everything was signed and made official for them to be stars of one of the episodes. Noticing that prices were spiralling a bit, and knowing the

The Con: Priscilla

family wanted to look as good as possible on TV, I offered to throw in a few extras.

After all, it would make Nico and my team look good to see the very best dresses we could do go out on air, so it made sense for me to be a bit more generous than usual.

I offered to fill in some of the diamanté patterns and provide bits like extra decoration for the bridesmaids' outfits – gloves, tiaras and so on. Eventually I even offered to do the mini-bride for nothing! This girl was going to get a significantly more expensive wedding than she was paying for, but I was happy to do it as they'd been great to deal with. It was all looking good – in every sense of the word.

A while later, after a lot of hard work from everyone on my team, the dresses were all ready, boxed up and awaiting collection. To see them all in the factory really was quite a sight – it took us almost a day just to pack everything up, there was that much of it.

Clearly it was going to take a pretty large van to transport it. Once it was done, Pauline and I stood back and gazed at the sheer volume of it, holding our cups of coffee and surveying what we'd come up with.

'Nice work,' I winked at Pauline. 'She's a lucky girl!'

Later that week, the family came to the factory to pick everything up. Well, not everything. As Pauline and I were booked to travel to Ireland to help dress Priscilla on the day, and because we were still making a few final tweaks, I said that they should come and get everything but the bride's dress itself.

This was quite normal as we always travel over in a big vehicle and often take the dress ourselves to make sure that it's safely stored right up until just before the wedding. Not everyone has room in their home to store a dress that size, whereas in the factory we've got the appropriate mannequins so it's really no big deal for us to do things that way. When I explained this to Priscilla's mum she seemed very relaxed about it. I asked her for the date and address of the wedding so that we could book our travel and make sure we were there with plenty of time, and everything seemed set.

Travellers are very secretive about their plans and often they don't like to reveal the details for the reception especially.

It had taken me a good few months to get these details out of the woman, but that didn't unnerve me any more now that she was planning for me to bring over the dress.

I was relaxed about everything and explained to her the way that we do things with the underskirts: as so many of the girls have the same shape to their dresses but the skirts providing that shape are never seen, we tend not to make fresh underskirts for each girl. Instead we ask for a sensible

The Con: Priscilla

deposit and then hire them out. This works really well as it keeps unnecessary costs down and also means that I don't end up losing underskirts all over the country!

When I explained this to Priscilla's mum, I let her know that I wouldn't be charging her a deposit as I usually do because we'd be bringing the skirts over ourselves and could then return with them the next day. They'd never be out of my sight, so why would I need the money to guarantee them?

The collection day came and the mother seemed more nervous than I had seen her before. For starters, she was insisting on taking away the bride's dress, despite what we had previously agreed.

'Her dad wants to see it,' she kept on insisting.

'But he'll see it on the day,' I reassured her. 'We'll get there the night before and then allow plenty of time for dressing Priscilla on the morning of the wedding, so it's not going to be a surprise to him.'

'No, he'll kill me if he can't see it when we get back tomorrow,' she repeated.

I looked at this woman, and I just knew that something wasn't sitting right. Her entire manner had changed. Something was up, I just didn't know what.

You must think I'm really thick, I found myself thinking, as I watched her chatting on and on about her husband. It seemed clear that they wanted all of the dresses but they didn't want me at the wedding. That meant that they didn't want the cameras, despite what they had agreed to, and all of the free work I'd done for them. A plan came to me.

75
The Con: Priscilla

'Well then, you'd best take it,' I told her with a gentle smile. 'We've not quite finished these gloves, though,' I added as a little test, 'so I'll be bringing them for you myself.'

'Ooh no! No, I want to take absolutely everything today,' she said. 'Even if I have to stay another day, I have to go back with everything.'

'It makes no sense,' I repeated to her. 'We'll be travelling with plenty of space, and not everything is ready right now, so we'll just bring it and save you the hotel costs for tonight.'

But she would not budge: she had to leave with everything, or she wasn't leaving. I wasn't sure about this at all.

The next day she returned and everything was loaded onto the van. While the mother was in the office sorting out the final payments, I grabbed Leanne and a couple of girls and whispered frantically to them: 'Go into that van right now and grab the boxes with the corsets in them. Go! Go, go, go! Hurry – and then hide them!'

They had no idea what I was on about or why they were being asked to do this, but I guess they trusted me well enough as by the time I returned to the office, I could hear them outside, scurrying back and forth in the van. But in all of the fuss in the factory and the slightly raised voices about the dress business, no one else – not Priscilla, nor her mother, nor the drivers – noticed the speedy to-ing and fro-ing from

The Con: Priscilla

my team. Key boxes were removed from the van so I knew the wedding could not go ahead without our cooperation.

They had been gone for about an hour when I started trying to call them to explain what I'd done, but every phone number I had for Mary was now a dead line and I had no other numbers for the family. We tried to phone the wedding venue that we'd been given but it was a dead line too and when we googled it, we realised there was no such wedding. In the meantime, the director from Channel 4 called the church where the ceremony was due to take place, only to be told that there was no wedding on that day.

We knew then without any doubt that we'd been given the wrong day and the wrong venue. As I suspected, the family had lied to me to so they could get free dresses and free work. I tried calling Priscilla's mum again and again; I tried all night. Nothing.

Then, about six the next morning, I got a call from her.

'I forgot the corsets,' she barked at me.

'No, you didn't,' I replied calmly.

'Yep, I did – I don't have them here,' she said.

'Yes, but you didn't forget them – I took them back,' I explained.

'Why would you do that?' she asked, suddenly sounding panicked.

'Do you really take me for a fool?' I said, refusing to let my voice waver.

'What do you mean?' she replied. 'What on earth do you mean?'

The Con: Priscilla

The Con: Priscilla

'You've given us the wrong venue, the wrong date – you've even given us the wrong town,' I replied calmly. 'I told you we were booking tickets to come out and dress your daughter – for free – and you were going to let us do that.'

'Oh no, there's just been a lot of chaos,' she blustered. 'I'm sorry if I got in a muddle about the dates. Why don't I come and get the rest of the stuff on Monday and we can sort it out then?'

'No problem,' I said, determined to remain calm.

Sure enough, she reappeared on the Monday. I was there, the show's director was also there, and we had a big sit down. We were given a definite time and date for the wedding, and she swore on her kids' lives that it was the truth. This time she had brought her husband with her, and he stood looking furious for most of the discussions. At one point he walked past me. 'You should be ashamed of yourself,' he muttered.

'Excuse me, why?' I replied.

'Making my wife have to come back here like that because you forgot to pack up half your dresses,' came his response.

It dawned on me that this poor man had no idea what his wife was up to – I couldn't believe the cheek of her!

'I think you need to have a talk with your wife,' I said, 'because there is no way that I am taking the blame for something that is totally her doing. I'd be annoyed too if that's what had really happened.'

In the end we decided we had got as far as we could with negotiations and that we just had to trust them. I'd done my absolute best with those dresses; we had all worked our socks off to create something really special for Priscilla, and for the viewers at home. But less than a week later I received a call from one of my other customers in Ireland.

'Listen, girls,' we were told. 'I understand that you're coming all the way out here to dress Priscilla.'

'Yes, yes, we are,' I replied, waving at Pauline and the others to come and listen.

'Well, I feel bad for you. I don't know why they're doing this but it's not right that you book tickets and make that journey for nothing.'

83

'What do you mean, "for nothing"?' I asked. My heart was beginning to sink as I realised our worst nightmare was coming true.

'I don't think you should come all the way here,' said the softly spoken woman. 'Because the wedding is definitely not taking place on that date, or at that place.'

'Thank you,' I said. 'I doubt we'll ever be able to find out when or where it is happening, but at least we won't make a wasted trip.'

I tried texting Mary: 'This is the address of the hotel we're staying in, see you there', 'Please text me back by 1pm today' and several other messages. But the lines went dead, and I couldn't get through to her. The wedding went ahead without my team's extra work ever being paid for, or even recognised. Although some of the confrontations were shown in the programme, Channel 4 were left with no wedding for the show and I never saw my underskirts again.

For weeks, I tried texting – I honestly said everything I could think of to get those skirts back, but nothing. Mary wanted something for nothing, and she made sure that she did what she had to do to get it.

Somehow it doesn't put me off, though. You'd think that being taken for a ride every now and again would stop me

The Con: Priscilla

trying to make gestures to please people, but I still find myself offering what I can, when I can. Will I ever learn? I always think that I'm never going to be shocked again by what some people will do, but then there's always another story to surprise me.

And not long after the fiasco of Priscilla and Mary, a girl called Chloe came in. She was a lovely girl; she just called and made an appointment, came down and had a nice chat with us. She told us quietly that while she wasn't a traveller, she was marrying one. She came in on her own, which was unusual in itself, but to be marrying in like that was a really big deal. I only know of a handful of girls who've done it.

Strangely she looked more like a traveller than an actual traveller, though – she had totally committed to the look. She had long, very dark hair and was very petite. She was pretty and she had really made an effort with her make-up and outfit – it was as if in converting she had gone the whole hog.

Having said that, she told us that while she wanted a proper gypsy wedding type of dress, she didn't want to go quite as flamboyant as some of the girls do. I'm not sure why – whether it was just her personal wedding style, whether she didn't want to make out that she was trying too hard to fit in, or whether she simply couldn't afford as much fabric given that she didn't have a traveller dad footing the bill.

When I say that she didn't want to be quite as flamboyant, I am of course being totally relative – we're talking traveller standards here. She was still having a very big dress.

Pauline took her order and drew out the designs with her and it all looked as if things were going to run smoothly. A while later she came by again to be measured up and to pay her deposit. While she was in the factory there was another girl's dress standing ready on a mannequin. It was enormous, with a huge skirt and the kind of curly frills that grow out of the dress, looking almost like sheer kale rather than the standard tulle that simply hangs from the waist. These curly skirts are what we in the factory call 'fish-wire skirts' as it takes a lot of wire to make those frills stand straight out; it requires several times more fabric to do it as well.

Chloe's eyes were well and truly caught by those fish-wire skirts and she asked how much they would be. Pauline explained how much extra work and materials the skirts took and that it was a lot dearer. But her heart was set on them, so they agreed the fish-wire skirts, as well as a couple more flowers to sit on the bodice of the dress. She left happy.

An hour later, though, she called back and said that while she still wanted the flowers, she would like to revert her order to the original, simpler tulle skirt.

'Maybe she can't afford them and she just got a bit carried away with the atmosphere in here,' I said to Pauline. That often happens and we try to keep an eye out for it.

'Maybe,' agreed Pauline, who seems to have learnt better than me to stop trying to get involved in what these girls are thinking and feeling.

So we forgot all about it.

When the time came to do Chloe's dress, I saw the drawing of the new skirt that had been discussed and cancelled. At Nico's I don't always remember every single girl. Once they've gone, I often forget who they are the minute that they walk out the door but in this instance that drawing reminded me of Chloe, and all the changes she was making in her life, and how much she wanted to be supported and accepted in her new community. I thought of her changing her mind later, and wondered what had done it when she'd seemed so set when she'd been in here.

'Oh, this is the kid who wasn't a traveller, isn't it?' I said to Pauline.

'Yeah, lovely she was,' Pauline replied. 'She wanted the other skirt and then changed her mind.'

'She came in on her own, didn't she?'

The Con: Priscilla

'Yes, yes, she did,' agreed Pauline.

Over the week we got on with making the corset and then, just as the skirt was about to be started, I had an idea.

'I tell you what,' I said to the girls. 'Do her the skirt she wanted – the larger fish-wire one.'

'Thelma, are you sure?' came the reply.

'Go on, let's just do it,' I said. 'We've got the fabric here in stock at the moment, and it does take a lot longer but it will be such a nice surprise for her.' So that's what we did.

A week or so later Chloe came to collect her dress. As was usual, it was there on display on a mannequin, just like the one that she had seen when she'd come to be measured.

I was still on my way back to the factory when she arrived, but apparently the first thing she said when she saw the dress was, 'That's not my dress, it has the wrong skirt.'

Pauline immediately realised that the girl was quite upset to have had her order overruled. Embarrassed at having to have a confrontation, she phoned me.

'She doesn't want the skirt, it's been a mistake,' she said.

'Oh no, that's such shame!' I replied. 'I really thought it would be a treat. But it's not a problem – we didn't do what she asked for so we'll have to do what she actually did order.'

When I walked into the factory a little while later she was there with her fiancé.

The Con: Priscilla

'Look, I am so sorry about this—' I began.

'Yes, Thelma just thought she was doing something nice for you, a bit extra,' continued Pauline. 'We really are sorry – we shouldn't have made that decision for you. But we'll sort it right away. We will do the skirt that you ordered. It is much simpler, so it won't take long. I just thought it would be a nice surprise.'

The girl was clearly upset, and caught between being polite and appreciating our gesture while panicking about not having the dress of her dreams. I felt dreadful to have put her in this position and really wanted to placate her.

But the boyfriend just looked at me. 'Yeah, but how much are you going to give us off?' he asked. 'We want compensating for this.'

I looked at Chloe, a bit startled to be honest. She seemed to know my intention had been good. While she was very determined that she did not want the skirt, she wasn't angry at all. I tried to talk to her, and she seemed to accept that this mix-up was a result of me trying to do a good deed, but he just kept interrupting and interrupting. It was rude and it was aggressive to a woman who had only tried to do something good.

In the end, I had had enough. I turned to him and said: 'What you basically want is money, isn't it? I tell you what, just leave the dress. You don't have to pay at all – I'll give you all your money back.'

Chloe was clearly very embarrassed, and felt stuck in the middle. 'No, Thelma, no – you don't have to do that!' she said.

'Look, we just want to know when you're going to deliver it,' he said. 'It's a 350-mile round trip, and we don't want to be doing it twice.'

'We'll work on this overnight,' I promised. 'If you can stay the extra night here in Liverpool, I'll pay, and then you can leave tomorrow with the dream dress.'

While her fiancé was speaking, Chloe barely said a word. She was a girl who had come in alone and ordered what she wanted; she seemed to have been paying for it, yet all of a sudden she wasn't saying anything at all, as if she'd learned her place. She just sat there and let him do all of the negotiating. I would address her and he would reply to me; I would ignore him and carry on trying to see if she was happy. It was bizarre.

The Con: Priscilla

'I'll have it ready for you this time tomorrow,' I said, 'and that's that.'

And that is what happened. As I stayed in the factory that night, working late on creating what this girl had asked for, I wondered if I was ever going to stop trying to give people something for nothing or finding them asking for it.

But I realised something else as dawn came up: it was a question of honour for that lad to have been going at me like that. It would have been such a sign of weakness for him to be letting people just do what they wanted with his bride-to-be's wishes. He had to be seen to be trying to defend his new wife's honour; to be trying his hardest.

What kind of an idiot would Chloe have thought she was getting, marrying into traveller life, only to have him go: 'Yeah, you're all right, don't worry about it' – and handing over a bundle of cash.

He was asserting his new position just as she would have wanted him to. She was stuck between two worlds, not just stuck between two skirts – and I hadn't made things any easier.

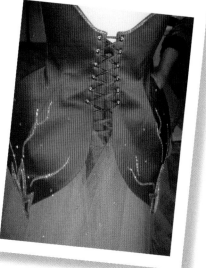

One day I'll learn, I keep telling myself. And I really hope I do.

The Con: Priscilla

CHAPTER FOUR

A Rathkeale Wedding

Lavinia

And when they say they're travellers, they really do travel. They all have houses – huge houses – in Rathkeale but they also have these massive trailers to go abroad in.

The thing that always keeps working with the traveller community interesting is the way there are so many smaller communities within it. After I'd seen the worst of their society a couple of times in people like Priscilla's parents and received a huge groundswell of support from travellers at other times, I started to think there was little left in the traveller community that could shock me. But that was before I'd seen a Rathkeale wedding. They are like nothing I had ever come across previously, and they're a community like no other.

A Rathkeale Wedding: Lavinia

In fact, the first time I did a Rathkeale wedding, I wasn't aware they were a different part of the travelling community.

It all started to dawn on me one spring a few years ago with a girl named Crystal. She had made an appointment and was one of the few traveller girls who arrived on the day of the appointment – a lot of them come anything up to two days either side of it. I knew she was a traveller because of the way that she spoke, but her accent was not exactly like the other travellers I had worked with. She had a very old-fashioned turn of phrase, calling her mother 'Mama' instead of 'Mammy', as I'd become used to. It was a very formal, almost prissy way of talking – she reminded me of something from *Little Women*. Crystal was underdressed for a traveller too, more countryside-ish than usual. She was in a cotton top with a higher neckline than I had seen other traveller girls wear and her skirt was below her knee. There were no shiny fabrics, no fancy hair or make-up; her nails weren't done either. It all seemed a bit more conservative, more natural. She had this schoolteacher vibe about her, even though she was very polite and she was a beautiful girl too, with gorgeous dark hair and properly classic Irish looks.

I didn't think there was anything to it when I met her, though, and just assumed that was her way. I wasn't sure if the family was particularly wealthy, as they didn't seem to be going out of their way to impress me with their bling in the way that some others do. With most families I know how far to go and what kind of thing they're after; whether it's about creating the dream to a budget or just about spending more

A Rathkeale Wedding: Lavinia

than the rest of their community. But this time I really didn't. My sense of judgment was very confused, especially when this girl chose a dress, paid a deposit with no question and left with a smile.

Having said that, though, the dress she ordered was no slouch in the glamour department. In fact, it was one of the flashiest creations we had done at that time. She wanted it to be decorated all over with the 'CD' of the Christian Dior logo. The whole thing was to be covered in 'Cs' and 'Ds', like a handbag. She wanted a matching bracelet and necklace, as well as a headpiece. The only thing that struck me as unusual was that she insisted on having a bolero jacket made as well, so that her shoulders were covered in the church. None of the other girls had ever asked for that – it felt like something from the 1950s. We were a smaller company then and we didn't think about the implications of copyright where the logo was concerned, so we just said 'OK' and got on with it. I was in the business of making these kids' dreams come true so I took the measurements and wished her well. The trouble was, we never heard from the girl again.

That's that, I thought to myself when we realised it was the first week of November and we'd had no word from the girl. She had told us that the wedding was for the 'twelfth month', an expression that a lot of the travellers use to describe when an event will take place.

They rarely give me the exact date of the wedding – presumably in case I tell someone else – but say, 'It's for either the tenth or eleventh month – I will let you know nearer the time.'

In Crystal's case I knew she meant December, and so time was pressing. We had opened the file for December dresses and were already working on them. For a few weeks we'd been wondering why she hadn't been in touch. All we knew was that she'd ordered this dress and we had ordered the materials to make it but we had heard nothing else. Usually the girls call or we give them a quick call before cutting into the fabric. The deposit we ask for doesn't even cover the materials so we always need to know that the dress is still wanted when we make a start on it, especially with a time

A Rathkeale Wedding: Lavinia

gap of about nine months, like this one. These days we are booked way ahead, but it was unusual then. It was all getting a bit late, and it seemed that she had given us a dead number.

We had tried and tried to get in touch, to the point where Pauline had started making a written note every time we made a phone call, just so there was some kind of record that it wasn't us who had forgotten the dress. 'Shall we do it, shall we not do it?' was starting to be a constant refrain running around my head every time I thought about this girl. The designs were all worked out and had been since she came in; we had her measurements, we had the fabric in stock. I had no reason not to trust her but she had vanished and that was really rare. Normally we can barely get a thing done for girls ringing to see how it's all going, but we hadn't heard from her since February and now it was early November: a decision had to be made.

Eventually I turned to Pauline and said, 'There's no point in making this dress. Surely anyone in their right mind would have been in touch by now – it's been months.'

We considered it a lucky escape – until a few weeks later. I was driving home one evening after I'd finished at the shop, a few days before Christmas, when my mobile rang. It was a bitterly cold night.

102

A Rathkeale Wedding: Lavinia

Snow was coming down and it was icy even as I was getting from the car to my front door. My phone was ringing again. I answered it. 'I'll be in tomorrow to pick my dress up,' the voice said. It was her.

'Hang on a minute, love,' I said. 'You are kidding me, aren't you? We haven't even cut the fabric as we haven't heard a dicky bird from you in months.'

'Yes, I know,' came the reply. Her voice was flat, as if she was totally unflustered. 'I've been abroad.'

'Jesus, that's one heck of a long holiday!' I said. I felt slightly hysterical – to me, it was all so crazy.

There was a pause on the line. It was like she was thinking, what's wrong with you? Why would you doubt me?

I took a deep breath and said what I had to say: 'I'm sorry, love, but it's not ready. We didn't know if you were ever coming back. We've been trying to call you for months and we've not had a thing back.'

She didn't even try to defend or explain herself; she seemed not to understand what I was finding so weird. But she wasn't throwing a diva fit either – she was still totally calm. I was not used to this.

'Well, in a week I've got to go back to Ireland,' she said. 'Could it be ready before I go?'

Again, that stillness in her voice – it made me almost admire her. This was a week before Christmas and the whole country was up to their ears in snow, mince pies and wrapping paper. I hadn't bought a single present, the tree hadn't been collected let alone decorated, and I knew I had a houseful of people coming over for Christmas dinner but I hadn't even begun to think about food. Like she cared.

'Listen,' I said. 'I've just got in. I want to help you, but you'll have to phone again tomorrow and we'll see what we can do.' It was the best I could offer but I'll admit I was intrigued, to say the least.

I couldn't wait for the girls to get into the factory the next morning. As soon as they did, I gathered them together and said: 'You're never going to believe who phoned last night.'

'Who?' said Pauline – the woman who's heard it all before.

'That girl – the one we've only been calling for weeks about the dress.'

'Go away!' At this Pauline sloshed tea on the table as she slammed her mug down in shock.

'And …' they leaned in to hear the punch line, 'she wants to come in and pick up the dress today!'

As I'd expected, the rest of the team were as gobsmacked as I had been. How come this girl had refused to take a call for the best part of a year and then expected us to have a completed dress for her the next day? Either way, we had taken the order and we had the materials there. We had even started on some of the basic bits we knew we could reuse if she hadn't shown. So we put our heads together and looked at everything that needed to be done. We realised that with a bit of overtime and by focusing only on that dress, we could do it. Just. But it would take a lot of time so close to Christmas, which wasn't fair on the team when we had already spent so long trying to find the girl.

It was Pauline who came up with the plan: if she wanted the dress done that fast, she would just have to pay for the overtime. It wasn't as if we hadn't tried.

'Tell her we'll stay and do it if she really needs it doing, but it'll cost her more,' said Pauline. 'And that's how we'll know if she's a crank or not.'

So I did, and all she replied was: 'If you need to charge me, charge me. But I'll be there next Friday to pick it up. No, actually, I'll send my dad.'

'Are you not going to try it on?' I asked, shocked (the final fitting on collection is usually such a huge part of the process).

'Oh no, I'm sure it'll be fine,' said the same old breezy voice. 'I'll just send my daddy to pick it up.'

She wasn't rude, but she wasn't especially grateful either. It was as if she never doubted this was how the situation would work itself out.

This girl was the complete opposite of any other bride I had ever worked with. I didn't hear from her for ten months,

she wasn't interested in trying her dress on or indulging in the traditional big fuss when she picked it up and she didn't care about the cost either.

'We'd like you to come in and try it on so we can make sure everything's perfect,' I said.

Now I was begging her to do something I usually found the most stressful part of the process but she didn't miss a beat. She just told me, 'My measurements don't change, they're always the same – it'll be fine.'

I hung up and told Pauline what I thought: 'We are never seeing this girl again. No way!'

But I was wrong: a week later her dad turned up, put the boxes in the back of his van, paid our fee in full, thanked us and off he went. While he was there we told him that he had to leave a deposit for the underskirts and he asked what that was for. We explained that we don't charge for making underskirts as we just loan them to the brides for the day.

'I'll just buy them, love,' was his deadpan response.

'Well, we don't sell them, you borrow them because we need them all the time,' I explained.

'OK, how much do you want?'

It was £500. He handed the money over with no further questions. We never saw those underskirts again. What's more, we never heard from that girl again – we were just left standing there after the dad had gone.

'What the heck was all that about?' I said to Pauline. 'Life would be easier if they were all like that to deal with, wouldn't it?'

With hindsight I must have been really thick because this went on for a couple more years before I realised a pattern was developing. That first bride was in 2005. Then the next year there were a couple more girls who came in the January but didn't reappear until mid-winter. One of them once made an appointment in about April and said: 'I'm coming with my aunt as she's coming back to England.'

I just thought, OK and didn't consider it any further. Then we started doing a lot of Communions, really expensive Communion outfits to the same timescale. Slowly I began to wonder. I can't even really remember when the penny dropped but the cogs definitely started whirring when, a while later, one girl asked me as I was fitting her: 'Have any other of our girls got one like this?'

Who are 'your girls'? I wondered. But I didn't have a clue and she was ordering something pretty unique so I just kept my head down on my tape measure and went, 'Oh nooooo!' and then wondered if I would ever find out what she was on about.

A week later, two giggling girls turned up together. The first one said to me, 'I'm marrying her brother and she is marrying mine so we don't have to pay a dowry – it's just a swap!'

A Rathkeale Wedding: Lavinia

'Ooh that's good, isn't it?' I replied, thinking, What are you on about? Dowries? For what? Didn't they go out of fashion in the Middle Ages?

They seemed chatty enough girls, so I decided to ask, 'So do you usually pay a dowry or something?'

They were great! The pair of them were about 17 or 18 and they explained that in their case everyone in both families was happy – the money that would have been put aside for a dowry would be saved for the next daughter.

At first they were going to have a double wedding but they didn't in the end as they realised how much fun they could have. I carried on asking them about the dowry business.

'Does the size of the dowry that has to be paid depend on what the girl looks like?' I asked. 'If it's a pretty girl do you pay less of a dowry?'

No, they explained, it all depended on the standing of the family within the community and where the boy is in that family. The bride's dad effectively had to make a compensation payment to the groom's family for the loss of a worker in the family business.

I carried on talking to them for long as I could string it out. It seemed like a different world, even compared to what I was already used to. I knew all about the travellers having a different culture from us, but this started to sound like another set-up altogether – these girls were turning up with their friends, not their mums and they never seemed to need approval on the finances at all. In so many other ways they were much more traditional than the travellers I was used to seeing, but they'd come in and order all this stuff – really going big on the dress and accessories – and I'd have to say, 'Look, I'm going to have to speak to your mum or dad about this.' But even when I tried to step in and make sure the costs didn't get out of hand, the answer that came back was always yes.

After doing a few more of these weddings, and chatting to a few other travellers, I came to realise that these people were all from Rathkeale, a small town in Limerick, Ireland, that is basically like the Hollywood of the travelling community.

And when they say they're travellers, they really do travel. They all have houses – huge houses – in Rathkeale but they also have these massive trailers to go abroad in. They take the whole family, and the whole family business – everyone goes and most of the town then gets shut up while they travel around for almost the whole year, from spring until just before Christmas. Honestly, if you go to Rathkeale in February, it's like a ghost town, all boarded up – there are bars on the windows and nothing to do at all.

From Spain to Eastern Europe and even America, they go all over the world. They keep moving, working and staying with their group.

Some of them are in antiques or reproduction furniture, some deal in wine, some run pony and traps, while others

A Rathkeale Wedding: Lavinia

are in construction. There really isn't one specific trade that they operate in, but they all work really, really hard and clearly do well out of it as this is a seriously rich community. To keep their wealth safe, they never, ever marry out of the community. They all grow up together too, which means they usually know who they will marry from an early age.

The dowry is all about keeping those businesses safe and running, as each firm will take a dent when a son leaves the nest to go and work with his new wife's dad. They've a smaller workforce so they can do less and need the money to make it up. The dads are buying an employee as well as their daughter's potential future happiness when they make that payment. For years we thought the families who would come in and mention how they had a big dowry to pay were just spinning me a line. We were convinced that they were trying to get out of paying full whack because we thought all travellers must be the same. Another family would come in and I'd ask: 'Do you pay dowries then as a matter of course?'

And they'd laugh at us, like it was a ridiculous idea: 'Do we heck!'
'I knew that last lot were lying!' I'd chuckle. Lots of the travellers have never heard of dowries, but the Rathkeale families really do pay them.

At the end of the year when the work is done, they all come back home and have a party season, which is like nothing you've ever seen before. Day in, day out, for a month or two it's back-to-back weddings, christenings and First Communions. The same people see each other for days on end, celebrating similar events. I came to realise that this is why the outfits mean so much to this community: if you're going to ten weddings in a row you've no chance of remembering the bride, let alone the mini-bride, the mother-of-the-bride or the bridesmaids if they don't wear something spectacular.

Also, the girls adopt this same, very conservative way of dressing throughout the rest of the year, especially once they are married, so these events are like a fashion bonanza. For them, it's a huge deal and they really go for it – hair, nails, make-up, the lot. The difference between their everyday look and their wedding day look is even more stark and pronounced than with a non-traveller bride, or even a regular traveller bride – it's almost the reverse of what they'll do for the rest of their lives. Despite this, they are all of such a particular body type and lifestyle that they are confident to order these dresses then leave the country for the rest of the year, safe in the knowledge that everything will fit when they come to pick it up.

A Rathkeale Wedding: Lavinia

It's amazing how relaxed about it most of them are as these girls go from a child to a woman in one day.

It's all very sudden and some of them are unbelievably young. They are given permission to marry by the local judge, who simply looks them up or down and makes up his mind based on what he sees. It seems a bit of a strange situation to me, especially as there has never been a rich Rathkeale girl refused permission in my experience.

You do notice how young these girls are sometimes, as they seem to be totally inexperienced in life. They're very excitable, very childish, and they have no sense of perspective. I remember Leanne once drew a sketch of a bridal crown for one girl as a demonstration of what she could do, and the girl looked up at her with worry sketched all over her face.

'It is going to be a bit bigger than that in real life, isn't it? I need it to fit properly,' she said, her finger brushing against the sketchpad.

'Yes love, that's just a picture,' Leanne explained.

Wow, I thought to myself, these really are sheltered girls! They are completely literal about everything. That's fine when they're dealing with the money or the practicalities as they've got no difficult side to them – they just get it sorted. But when it comes down to trying to describe the shape of a petal or a flower, or even the type of fabric we could use for

A Rathkeale Wedding: Lavinia

a dress, often they just don't get it. You mention a rose and they simply can't call the image of a rose to mind, so Leanne has to get drawing again – making sure that she points out whether or not it's to scale.

Whether it's Disney or TV stars or dolls, these girls have the same references as other girls, but they have no experience of the world outside their community.

The girls are literally just inside those trailers, keeping them spotless while they travel the world, and yet somehow seeing none of it. Nevertheless, this is a really respected community. The formal way that they have of speaking is like a kind of poshness – they are unique. But I didn't understand this until I actually visited Rathkeale myself for the first time.

A few years after Crystal's wedding, while I was still making sense of this community, her sister Lavinia came in and said she'd like to order a wedding dress too. Straight away, she told us that we had worked with her family before and I recognised her slim and petite, almost elf-like features as being the sister of Crystal; she had the same chatty and confident nature too. She was also 16 or 17, the same age as her sister had been when she first came to me.

It was great to hear that they weren't an unknown lot. Lavinia told us that when she was getting married there were

The dresses for the Night Before Parties are always vibrant colours, with everyone trying to stand out as best they can. Basically, these are parties where the girls are trying to find husbands so they wear very elaborate outfits and have as much skin on show as possible, and as much sparkle and colour as the remaining fabric can take. They're like birds of paradise or tropical birds, fluttering around the object of their desire.

Often the dresses are long at the back, with a glamorous train, and then short at the front to show off the girl's legs. They all seem to have amazing figures so it's something they want to make the most of, especially as they dress so conservatively the rest of the time.

The fabrics they want for these dresses are often influenced by their travel in southern Europe, with a bit of a La Isla Bonita vibe. These families are sometimes in Spain for a year at a time and the girls will come back with a taste for that Flamenco dancer look – that's definitely how the pineapple and the palm tree ideas came about.

The Night Before Parties usually start at about 7pm and are almost always held in a club called Davy Mac's. There is a buffet and music and dancing. The girls all adore the dancing, often playing with little siblings and cousins, and some of the older girls start to flirt with the boys. During the event the men tend to do a lot of business, chatting about money and plans while they're back in town. It's a big boozy night for them too – they really put it away. But not for the girls, who don't drink at all.

A Rathkeale Wedding: Lavinia

Then the next morning the bride is up early, getting her hair and make-up done, being strapped into her dress and spending time with her family and sisters. It's a big female 'bosom-of-the-family' type scene.

The men just get up with their hangovers, put on a shirt and tie and go to the pub for a hair of the dog – and the rest. The girl's family is not usually so bad and will often stay in the house, running around and tending to her. But as for the groom and his family … that first time I had no idea!

Cherry Girl's wedding was the first time we had been over to Rathkeale to dress a bride and that year we had four of them to do.

We were still getting our heads around the whole system of the season and the Night Before Parties but we hadn't reckoned on the drinking.

Luckily we didn't get involved as we were too busy making last-minute tweaks to Lavinia's wedding dress and had an early start the next morning but we've been to a few now and I can tell you, it's quite an experience!

I got to the house bright and early to begin helping Lavinia to get ready. Knowing it was her big day, she was milking the attention from her family for all it was worth. She really looked gorgeous, though.

A Rathkeale Wedding: Lavinia

The cherry motif worked a treat – the dress was asymmetrical and had the fruit coming over one shoulder as well as sparkles shooting across the bodice itself.

Her skirt was what we call a 'Christina skirt', as that was the name of the first girl we made it for. It's the one with the material going almost horizontally, creating really curly frills coming out of the dress rather than hanging straight down like regular tulle. It's a trade secret how we make them, but they always create a massive effect – and so they should because they use twice as much fabric and we have to make each bit by hand!

As with all Rathkeale weddings, the service was booked for midday but when we got there, there seemed to be a lot of standing around. Lavinia was there, looking gorgeous, but her groom was nowhere to be seen. Pauline and me were standing at the side of the church, observing this waiting game with fascination.

I was scanning everyone's faces, trying to gauge some kind of reaction there. No one seemed to be panicking, though. The bride herself appeared perfectly calm – she was even on her phone at times, chatting away.

Had it been an ordinary wedding I would have imagined the bride starting to freak out by now, her arms windmilling and brows fraught – especially as this was a cold mid-winter's day and she was in a strapless dress, shivering in the snow. But no, it was like she didn't care at all. On top of this, the TV cameras for the show were around.

'This girl is about to be humiliated in front of the nation,' I muttered to Pauline, who was beginning to look as concerned as I was. 'Why is no one even doing anything? It's so cruel!'

More and more people started to stream into the church. It was the middle of the wedding season and the whole town was coming. Everyone in their finest, wishing each other well.

The Channel 4 crew were there, catching it all, but still no groom. I was really freaking out now, but the bride didn't seem at all bothered. She and her family were just standing there as if nothing was wrong. Surely it was just a front? Someone had to do something.

Eventually I plucked up the courage to stick my oar in and so I went over to the family to ask was what going on.

I tried to be discreet; I just wanted to do the right thing by the girl while the camera crew was there – I didn't want to see a bride humiliated on my first trip to Rathkeale either. But the family seemed genuinely surprised when I expressed my concern.

A Rathkeale Wedding: Lavinia

'Oh no, love,' explained one of her aunties. 'He's in the pub.'

'What do you mean – he's in the pub? He's meant to be getting married!' I whispered to her.

She seemed curious as to why I'd even asked – 'It's tradition, love. Nothing to worry about.'

'But she's just standing there, freezing!'

'I know, love, but he'll get here.' She seemed to be trying to hush me up now. I was gobsmacked. 'That's just what we do here – we try to keep the groom in the pub as long as possible.'

And it turns out they do. With every wedding there's a sort of competition to see how late the groom can be. It runs for the whole wedding season, with the lads trying to keep their mates in the pub for as long as possible. They're doing it on purpose; it's a question of honour rather than simply wanting to get the beers in. It all depends on what family the groom is from and his standing in the community. Some of these lads really love their bride and want to get to the wedding while others are really cocky because they know they're from a respected family and everyone will just have to wait for them. It's an act of bravado, trying to keep the bride's family on their toes, so the bride and her family are used to letting the situation unfold how it will.

I have since been to one Rathkeale wedding where the groom got so drunk that he had to have other lads holding him up in the church just to get through the service.

He knew he could get away with it, that he was worth a big dowry and her family would take it. I felt sorry for that

A Rathkeale Wedding: Lavinia

123

A Rathkeale Wedding: Lavinia

bride but at the end of the day she felt she had got herself a good catch and that was that.

This particular groom did turn up eventually, and he made sure we all knew it. Drivers were beeping their car horns all the way along the street to the church – everyone was dangling out of the windows, waving and hooting like proper lads. But the fun didn't end when they parked up – the boys just got out of their cars and started larking about in the snow. They were all there in their tuxedos but started throwing snowballs at each other, having fights and even peeing up against the side of the church.

The bride can't go into the church until the groom is already in there and up the aisle, so this girl had to stand there – almost blue with cold – while they carried on rolling around in the snow until they were done.

Things didn't seem to get any more relaxing when the ceremony began as the service was so austere. There was

A Rathkeale Wedding: Lavinia

no music in the church, absolutely none. That poor girl, looking so beautiful, having gone to all that effort and then having to walk down the aisle to no music at all.

Then, when the priest starts talking you've got people walking in and out of the church, lads getting up and going off to the bathroom. And it's not as if the ceremony is informal: it's full mass – a long service, even if you've cut all the hymns out. Nonetheless the entire congregation just carries on doing exactly what they want, while the priest, used to these weddings, carries on oblivious, with the bride and groom at the front, trying to get married!

After the ceremony we drove through ice and snow for four hours to the reception and when we got there, the hotel was clearing up. The bridal party had only arrived about half an hour before we did, and now they were ready to leave.

The wedding dress was shortly to be taken off and replaced with another slim-fitting skirt to carry on partying. The cycle was starting all over again.

A Rathkeale Wedding: Lavinia

That first Rathkeale wedding left me with a massive sense of anticlimax. I was stunned at the way they had behaved, but now I can see that it is simply their way of life. I understand that for them it's one of the reasons why the dress is such a huge part of getting married. Realistically, if you're a girl of marriageable age in Rathkeale you'll need about 30 new elaborate dresses for the couple of weeks around Christmas.

In a way the process of getting the wedding dress made is as important as the day itself.

Part of the experience of becoming a wife is provided by us at Nico. In some ways it's almost as if I officiate in the process myself. The girls know each other – they all go to the same club the night before, they go to the same church. The only thing that is different is the dress.

A Rathkeale Wedding: Lavinia

CHAPTER FIVE

The Bride
Who Couldn't Decide

Sabrina

There she was, drenched, and a bit in shock. And having to do that long walk up the aisle in a state none of us would ever want to be seen in, let alone on a day we'd been planning for so long.

*S*ome brides come and go without me getting to know them at all. But others … well, there are brides whose ceremony I end up becoming an actual part of. In the case of Sabrina, I was to play my most prominent role yet. Sabrina first came to see me in the summer of 2011, but she had been planning for her wedding since the January before. She wasn't a Rathkeale girl, she was from Galway, but as with the Rathkeale girls, I was booked to go out to dress her.

The Bride Who Couldn't Decide: Sabrina

We nearly didn't make it to the big day, though, let alone down the aisle. She first came into the shop with her sister and her sister-in-law. They were both married, and a bit older than her. Sabrina was 23, so older than the average traveller bride herself. But by non-traveller standards she didn't look old to be a bride. A pretty girl, with blonde hair and a cute nose, she had lovely tanned skin and pale blue eyes – the kind of colouring that can look great in a white, sparkling dress. But it wasn't her looks that stood out – it was the fact that she simply couldn't make a decision. In all my years of dealing with brides I have never seen anything like it and I doubt I ever will again. She took the whole idea of bridal indecision and turned it into something of an art form.

It began with the first appointment. She turned up for her first meeting unannounced, when I was heading out to do some filming. I said I wouldn't be back until about 9pm but she said she would wait. I assumed she wouldn't do that, but sure enough, when we got back at 9.30, she was waiting outside the shop, standing against the wall. It was hard not to admire her persistence.

So we got her into the shop and began chatting to her but pretty soon it appeared that all she wanted to discuss was that we'd come back with her to Ireland to do the dress on her wedding day. She had seen the show on TV and it was a big deal for her that we were going to be making her wedding dress. From the moment she sat down she was adamant that we would go back to Ireland with her and dress her on her wedding day – less because she wanted to have

The Bride Who Couldn't Decide: Sabrina

me sorting out the dress and more because she thought that no one would believe she was getting her wedding dress from Nico.

Every five minutes she kept saying it: 'You will come back, won't you? You will come back? You're coming back, aren't you?' We said yes, and we meant it. But then came the challenge of the dress itself.

We sat her down with a cup of tea and said what we usually do to the girls: 'So, have you got any ideas?' At this point the girls often have printouts of princess dresses, Disney characters or dolls that they want to copy. Sometimes they even have doodles of their own that they have kept since before they were teenagers and have always dreamt of having turned into a reality. These scrapbooks and ideas are a rite of passage, something the girls have been working on long before they find a husband. But this time: nothing.

She looked at us, blank, sighed and said: 'Noooooo!'

Now it's nearly ten o'clock at night, we've all been working all day; we were all absolutely shattered. We were trying to lead her through the process, to draw her towards some

The Bride Who Couldn't Decide: Sabrina

sort of thoughts about a wedding dress, but it was like getting blood out of a stone. 'Do you want a bodice?' we'd say, and her sisters would look at us, then at her and say, 'Is that what you want, Sabrina?' There would be a long pause while she seemed to think and then she would say back at us, 'What do you think?' as if it wasn't us who had just asked her.

We were going nowhere. Every time I suggested something to her, she would look around at her sisters and us. 'Yeah?' she'd go. Then, if we suggested something entirely different to be sure what she'd said yes to was what she really wanted, she would do exactly the same thing. It was as if she wanted to give the right answer, each and every time without knowing it was up to her and her alone to decide what that right answer should be. My patience was beginning to fray.

'I don't know what you want, love,' I said. 'You're going to have to help me here – I don't know what's in your head.'

The Bride Who Couldn't Decide: Sabrina

That first night I assumed she was overawed, that she couldn't believe she was in the shop that had been shown on the TV, that perhaps she had nervous excitement and was all aflutter. That's what we all thought, as we sat there for two and a half hours, talking to her. But we just couldn't get anywhere.

Everything I asked her, time and again, she would look at her sister so that she could answer on her behalf. Eventually I came to realise that she had been dependent on having older sisters all her life and this was her breaking-away point.

She was very quiet, very nervous of it; she had no concept of her own independence or how to use it so she was in entirely new territory.

In the end I realised nothing was going to get done that evening so I asked if she was planning to stay in Liverpool for the night. When she said she was, I said: 'I tell you what, go and have a good night's sleep and come back in the morning. You'll be nice and fresh and we can go over everything then. We'll measure you up and start the whole process again from scratch.'

Now that I'd made a decision for her, she was very obedient and off she went. At 9am she was back in the

The Bride Who Couldn't Decide: Sabrina

office. I'd had some sleep, she had had some sleep – I was sure things would be different. She had to get the plane back at midday, so I gave her a firm 'OK!' and we gave it a second shot.

At 11.30am she had still not made one single decision after two and a half hours of talking, ideas and drawing out suggestions for her and so on. Nothing was decided. Whatever we tried only seemed to confuse her more. We knew this was a big wedding – she was also having three bridesmaids and a

The Bride Who Couldn't Decide: Sabrina

mini-bride, all from me – so it wasn't as if she was trying to budget or hesitating over costs. Often a girl will just have her dress from me and then get the dresses for her bridesmaids elsewhere to spread the load but Sabrina wanted everything matching, and everything from me. But that was all she knew: she had no idea about the rest.

It's Leanne or me who does the drawings for the girls while they're here in the factory. At first it was always me, but now it's more often Leanne. On this occasion she was in the corner all morning, sketching at the speed of light with the pencil going and the rubber scratching away. She was flipping through the sketchbook, becoming more and more anxious, her wrist getting sore and little flecks of rubber flying around. Leanne's not the subtlest person when she's under pressure – she makes me look really delicate. She was starting to say 'What? Do you know what? How am I supposed to know what you want if you don't tell me?' and Sabrina would sit there smiling and looking totally confused.

She was just having a traditional bodice and a skirt, but it was the details – the embellishments and the fabrics – that were causing the problem. Did she want organza? What sort of a veil? Diamanté or crystals? What colour for the bridesmaids? These are all things that other girls usually have had in their heads for years. Sabrina was a lovely girl but I couldn't believe just how little she seemed to mind – she just wanted to please everyone else. There was no malice in her, and she wasn't deliberately making a scene or attention-seeking, but it didn't make the process any less frustrating.

The Bride Who Couldn't Decide: Sabrina

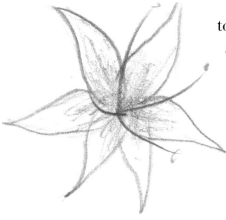

Eventually we nudged her towards making some decisions about the dress and all the details, only for her to announce that she wanted to come back again another day to try everything on. This wasn't usual and I knew that if we allowed her to do this it had the potential to make her change her mind about everything she had at last decided on all over again.

Normally, when the bride-to-be arrives for her first appointment she has her clutch of ideas, we do some sketches of what we can create, we take her measurements and a deposit, and then she's off again.

Unless there are changes to the design we don't tend to see or hear from them until it's time to collect the dress. On that day they come in early for a final fitting. They're here first thing in the morning, they try the dress on and we agree any alterations or size modifications that need to be made before they head off into town for a while. They have a nice lunch, get their nails done or whatever they fancy, and we do what needs to be done on the dress. These are big days for the team here; it's a long session and we're in early to make sure all hands are on deck. No one goes home until the bride goes home. It's exciting, but it can be potentially chaos.

This time I was really worried that Sabrina would change everything we had just decided on if she came back for an extra fitting. I said she didn't need to come back, but she was sure she'd need to. She wanted to come on something like 19 or 20 December, when I knew we'd be frantic with

Rathkeale girls but in the end I said OK – I think I just wanted her to stop talking about it and relax! We'll deal with that situation when we come to it, I told myself. I didn't even have to wait that long.

Almost as soon as she had got off the plane, Sabrina phoned and said she wanted to make all kinds of changes to the dress. It was only then that she told me she'd missed her first flight because she'd been in the shop for so long.

And then she was back on the phone again from 10am until 7pm the next day, going over the same things we'd talked about the first time we met. After hours – literally hours – of patient coaxing, I got her to stick to one plan so that we could get on with ordering materials and planning our time.

One thing I was really relieved to know when dealing with Sabrina was that the travellers from Galway all have a very specific, quite breathy way of speaking. A few years ago I didn't know that it was a regional thing rather than an emotional one. Because this accent makes them sound very nervous, even when they're not that anxious. For the first few times I dealt with these women I thought they were on

The Bride Who Couldn't Decide: Sabrina

the edge of a nervous breakdown but after a while, after I'd met their mums and their sisters and done a few weddings with the community, I found myself thinking, they can't all be living on the edge, can they? Sure enough, I chatted to a few about it and realised it was just their way. If I hadn't known this about Sabrina then I'm not sure that I could have handled that volume of phone calls. By the end of the week I had decided that humour was the only way to cope with her, so I started with some teasing.

'Hiya love, how are you feeling today?'
I'd say.
'Well, you know …' she'd start.
'Nice and decisive?' I'd chuckle.
'Um …'
'I thought so – I knew I could count on you!'

She took it well and I started to hear her giggling on the end of the line. Finally, we were getting somewhere.

I came up with a masterplan to go and visit Sabrina in Ireland while we were there for the Rathkeale weddings, to save her the trouble of coming over again. By the time we got to Galway it was to be the fourth time we were seeing her, which is pretty much unheard of at Nico – especially as we hadn't even cut into a single piece of fabric yet. Any guesses why? Yes, she just kept changing her mind! In the end we were in a hotel lobby with her, trying to get her to calm down and make a final decision. The fabric had to be cut. We really had to spell it out to her that this was the final moment for decision-making.

'Right, Sabrina,' I said, looking her square in the eye. 'This is it! You're going to have to make your mind up once and for all before these scissors get moving. Are you happy with this plan?'

'Yes,' she replied in that familiar whisper. 'Yes, I think so. Yes, I think I am. What do you think?'

'It doesn't matter what I think,' I told her. 'I am here for you. It's what you think that matters, isn't it?'

'Yeah,' she said. It was barely a whisper now.

I had to accept that this was a very nervous girl in a new situation that she was actually finding quite difficult. We had to take her word, and just get on with making a dress. And so we did.

The day she came to collect the dress I was at another wedding so I was out of the office. It was another great day for Pauline! I wasn't even in Liverpool, but that didn't stop me from having the full experience as far as the day went. My phone did

The Bride Who Couldn't Decide: Sabrina

not stop ringing. Every five minutes Pauline was on my mobile with a new question or something to run by me. Just the process of getting everything into the boxes and out of the factory proved a total nightmare, a never-ending nightmare. Sabrina was still trying to canvass opinion and make changes even though the dresses were finished; she didn't bring enough money with her and she had to sort out payments in total chaos.

When the day of the wedding finally arrived our relationship had stopped being about me trying to get a decision out of her, and more about me trying to keep us both laughing.

I felt like I was going mad, I know Leanne felt the same and we were both pretty sure that Sabrina herself was close to buckling under the pressure of trying to please everyone with no idea how to go about it. To everyone's relief we unearthed a sense of humour in the girl, though. Every single time we had to get a decision out of her, her instinct would be to look at either her sister or one of us in the shop and to start her usual refrain: 'What do you think?'

The sisters would try and answer but I'd cut them off.

'It doesn't matter what anyone else thinks, love – it's your dress!'

'I know, but I just want—'

'What? What do you want, love? We are all dying to know!' I'd say.

She'd fold into giggles again and shrug at me, rolling her eyes in despair at herself.

'I'm so sorry, Thelma. I'm not trying to be difficult, I just want everything to be perfect.'

Sabrina really had started to grow up and come out of herself a bit by the end. She was still changing her mind right up until the last minute, though, calling me days before the event to say, 'I want my dress bigger.'

'You couldn't even move in it when you were here in the studio!' I told her. 'How on earth are you going to manage something even bigger?' There was the traditional pause and then she sounded sure.

'Yeah, I know I couldn't move, but I definitely want it bigger. Can you do something?'

'Well, we'll bring some more underskirts,' I offered, surprised by her new certainty. 'Packing extra underskirts is not a problem, so we'll just see how you go on the day.'

As I made a note to pack up four extra sets of underskirts with the dress I realised that despite myself I was looking forward to seeing Sabrina when we set off for Galway and the big day.

The Bride Who Couldn't Decide: Sabrina

As soon as we got to Sabrina's home we could see that she came from a lovely family. On the way there, Leanne – who, as a qualified hairdresser, had offered to do her hair for the day – and I had quite a chat about how close we'd become and how fond of her we were now. We just wanted all her efforts to be worth it on the big day. We could immediately see that her indecision was a result of coming from a very loving, protective family rather than any intention to be manipulative – I don't think she could have been manipulative if she'd tried! We were welcomed into the home with open arms and I really, really wanted her to have a lovely day.

But as the day dawned there was an immediate sign that things might not run entirely smoothly: the weather was horrendous. It was gale-force winds in Galway, to the point where it was stressful and even felt dangerous driving to the house and getting our kit out of the car. It was awful, just awful, and I had a real sense of dread that this was going to make things harder for Sabrina. Leanne and I exchanged worried glances and headed in, doing our best to be cheery and professional. The dress was only half on by the time Sabrina started to whimper and moan in pain. Like a lot of traveller brides, she had decided to wear trainers underneath the skirts to at least keep her feet pain-free (the multiple skirts and tiny corset were another matter). Just as I'd warned, she was finding the weight and the tightness very sore, though.

'Ouch, ouch! I didn't realise,' she was yelping.

'These are not even the extra skirts, love,' I told her. 'Do you think you still want them?'

The Bride Who Couldn't Decide: Sabrina

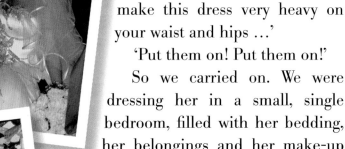

'It's really hurting but I do!' came the surprisingly decisive reply.

'Are you sure? It's going to make this dress very heavy on your waist and hips …'

'Put them on! Put them on!'

So we carried on. We were dressing her in a small, single bedroom, filled with her bedding, her belongings and her make-up plus other kit for the wedding. Leanne and I were standing above her on the bed, trying to strap her in, and in the remaining few inches of space in the room there was a succession of excited small children peeking in to get a look at the drama.

Just outside the door there were drinks being opened and people were arriving, and a constant stream of family members were all trying to pop in for a favour.

'Oh Thelma, could you help me with my hat?'

'Oh Leanne, could you just help me adjust this?'

'Ladies, do you think you could let me know what you think I should do about this?'

The heat was rising and Sabrina was starting to look very flustered. I just wanted to protect her, to get her safely to the church to enjoy her special moment. That was when the final surprise came.

'Sabrina, love, will you look out of the window? Your mum and dad have got a special treat for you!' said one of the many passing relatives.

All three of us leaned out of the window and there it was: a tiny Morgan sports car. The classic old-fashioned two-seater in cream was gleaming in the torrential rain. It was an amazing car, waiting for her, with its own special driver. If you've ever seen a Morgan you'll know that you can barely fit one person in them, let alone two, one of whom is wearing one of my dresses. There was a flutter of excitement among the family in the house and Sabrina herself squealed with excitement. I just looked at the car, and at her, then back at the car. How the hell is this going to work then? I thought to myself.

We had made this beautiful creation of a girl – it had taken months and months. The coaxing, the teasing and the building up of her confidence to get every last detail and decision out of her but now she looked gorgeous, absolutely stunning. The dress itself was huge, definitely one of my biggest creations once the extra skirts were added. Before she took the extra skirts the dress weighed 16 stone so I can't begin to imagine what it was once she was in all of them.

There were bales and bales of fabric, the hoops to support the skirts and 18 packets of crystals – that's like wearing the weight of a man, or a man and a bit!

And she had a whole jungle on it as she hadn't been able to choose between designs and had ended up with several. There were palm leaves, almost a whole tropical forest of them. Honestly, everything you could think of was on this dress, every type of decoration and a proper jungle's worth of foliage! There were 30,000 Swarovski crystals on those patterns. And she had really maintained a sense of humour as we had got hotter and hotter in that room. By the time she was ready we were exhausted after hours spent rammed in there, trying to tie and tweak and get the entire outfit looking perfect. She hadn't liked her hair so Leanne had redone it, adjusting her crown and the tumbling curls that she had coming down around her shoulders. Her make-up was quite subtle compared to some other brides I've worked with, but it was still perfectly applied, with lovely glossy lips.

The Bride Who Couldn't Decide: Sabrina

When I saw the car I just knew there was trouble ahead. Then the horizontal lashing rain began. Even if it had been a fabulous, gorgeous sunny day there was no way that car would have been a good idea. But the chorus behind us was growing.

'Ooh, do you like your present?' they were asking, keen to see her excitement but not taking into consideration the practicalities. The entire family was so excited and Sabrina herself was made up to have a treat that she hadn't had to decide for herself.

Leanne and me were just looking at each other, thinking, What the f*** is going on here, and how are we going to avoid getting involved?

We were staying in the hotel where the reception was to be held and we'd known instantly that this was going to be a beautiful event. And the more we had heard throughout that morning, the more we realised that it would be a massive wedding.

The Drifters – the actual Drifters – as well as a stunning Elvis impersonator and even a Michael Bublé impersonator were singing at the reception. But getting to the church was the one thing no one seemed to have thought through.

The Bride Who Couldn't Decide: Sabrina

'Don't even go downstairs,' I told Leanne when we saw that car pull up, 'because then it'll be down to us to sort this out, and it's just not our problem.'

We made ourselves look very, very busy and avoided all eye contact as we tidied up our belongings and made a note of the many extra underskirts Sabrina had eventually got into. As we gathered together the bits we'd need for the reception – hairspray, shoes and whatever else we'd have to have to hand – we made ourselves unavailable to the wedding party in our busyness.

We could see them from the windows at the front of the house as they began the attempt to fit Sabrina into the sports car. It was like something from a mad caper movie.

What the family came up with, after a lot of consideration and chat, was for Sabrina to sit with her feet in the leather well of the passenger seat, her bum and skirts on the back of the car. The dress spilled over almost all of the rest of the car, so the driver looked as if he was drowning in skirts. There was dress everywhere and then two heads and four wheels! On a dry day this might have been a laugh, but the poor girl was sitting there in the lashing wind, with rain coming straight at her from what looked like all angles. It really was awful.

The Bride Who Couldn't Decide: Sabrina

Once she was off, we got into our car and followed her. It was not a pretty sight. In all my career I have never, ever felt so sad for a bride.

The poor girl! I didn't care about the dress any more – it was made – but I also knew how much effort had gone into it on her part. It had been a real struggle to make those decisions and for the weather to be like that just seemed real cruelty on fate's part. It must have been the worst weather in history that day – honestly, recordbreakingly bad. And there she was, sitting on top of this car and getting drenched because of an attempt at a kind surprise from her family. It broke my heart, it really did.

By the time she arrived at the church her veil was totally stuck to her face with the imprint of her features on the fabric itself, and she was windswept beyond belief.

The skirts were soaking wet too, now just comprising a load of sodden tulle dragging her down.

Everything you can ever think of that happens when you come in from being caught out by a rain shower, but all at once it was happening to her, and on her biggest day too.

The dress hadn't been able to sit straight on the car because obviously the hoops had to go somewhere so it naturally sat at an angle. This in turn meant that some parts of the skirts had soaked up more water than others, making

The Bride Who Couldn't Decide: Sabrina

them heavier and pulling the entire dress down at all the wrong angles. I wanted to dry her off, to give it a bit of tender loving care and to give Sabrina herself a cuddle and a word of reassurance. I felt so sorry for her, after all that effort, but it wasn't our place. We did our best and went into the church.

It was a massive, massive wedding – there were hundreds of guests in there, all waiting to have their first glimpse of the glorious bride.

She still looked beautiful, but she was drenched, and a bit in shock. And having to do that long walk up the aisle in a state none of us would ever want to be seen in, let alone on a day we'd been planning for so long. At least no one will forget this wedding, was the best I could think of to try and persuade myself there was an upside to the situation.

The ceremony seemed as if it would be gorgeous. There was an absolutely lovely performance of 'Ave Maria' and the priest was leading the service towards the vows. Then, suddenly, Sabrina turned round and looked straight at me. I didn't understand. 'Is she looking at us?' I whispered to Leanne.

I was looking behind me to see if there was someone else due in the church. Maybe that was what she was looking at. But she looked again – I was so confused. Then her mother came over.

'Thelma ...' she whispered.

You are joking ... I thought to myself.

'She wants your help, Thelma. She says her skirts are hurting.'

'I know,' I replied. 'I told her they would.'

'She wants you to take some of the skirts off.'

'But she's actually getting married now!' I whispered back to her.

'It doesn't matter. Because she really wants you to go and take some of those skirts off,' she replied.

Sabrina had actually gone up the aisle and then halfway through her own vows she had decided she wanted me to come and take away half the dress. We were talking about interrupting the actual 'do you take this man' moment – I could not believe it.

She looked around again. Her husband was there, standing right next to her, so who else could she be looking for?

'You want me to go now?' I said to the mother. 'She's got 150 people looking at her ...'

'Yeah.'

'She is actually getting married! Let's give it five minutes, shall we. I'll do it in a minute ...'

'OK, only five minutes, mind.'

The Bride Who Couldn't Decide: Sabrina

And less than five minutes later the girl had looked round at me all over again. Oh my God! I was thinking. She did not stop turning, looking more and more distracted.

'I now pronounce you man and wife ...' said the priest and, without missing a beat, she said, 'Thelma, come here!'

I got up and went towards her as discreetly as I could but she was already pleading in front of everyone:

'Thelma, please, please – I beg you, I beg you! Take this off me! Take this off me!' Every single one of the guests was watching.

'Everyone's staring,' I said. 'We'll go outside.'

'No!' she interrupted. Her voice was rising now. 'No, no, no! I can't make it outside – I won't make it!'

'OK, don't panic,' I told her. 'We'll just have to wait for everyone to go outside themselves then.'

'No! I need you to do it now! I need you to do it!'

'But we're standing at the altar,' I whispered, still desperate to be try to be subtle, but we'd passed the point of no return.

The poor fella was left standing there at the altar and everyone else at the wedding was left sitting there listening

The Bride Who Couldn't Decide: Sabrina

to another hymn while I had to walk up the aisle myself, pull Sabrina behind the altar and dive under her dress to start taking off her skirts.

It was like a kind of performance art – Sabrina had got the lady from the TV show to come to her wedding and now she wanted to make me do something in front of her congregation. Leanne was there too, burrowing up under the skirts, while Sabrina wept – 'The pain! The pain!' – like a grieving widow.

We managed to get one, maybe two off, and reassured her that we would do more at the hotel. The priest and the congregation were just staring in shock; everyone saw everything, and no one knew what to do. Obviously this had never happened before. The same situation greeted us when we got to the hotel for the reception. Sabrina was waiting in the lobby, shrieking,

'Thelma, Thelma! Help me!'
'Come on, let's go upstairs and get this sorted,' I said, on seeing her.
But she simply cried even more. 'No! Now! Just do it here – I can't take it!'

'This place is full of people,' I said, 'we can't do it here!'
'Yes, we can – I can't take any more pain!'
'You're the one who wanted me to bring four more skirts,'

The Bride Who Couldn't Decide: Sabrina

I said. 'Now do you understand why I said no, that it was going to be too heavy for you to take?'

But there was no reasoning with her: we had to take the skirts off, there and then.

But within half an hour it had turned into an absolutely fantastic wedding. With all those acts playing, the dancing was incredible and Leanne and I were invited to take part in the meal too. It was a proper sit-down meal – no expense spared – with three courses, steak, linen napkins and delicious wine and puddings.

Work or not, it really was one of the loveliest weddings I have ever been to. They were the nicest people you could wish to meet, every single one of them, and they really went out of their way to make us feel welcome and part of the day's celebrations.

Sabrina herself seemed thrilled that the room was filled with so many happy people. She had done so much to try and keep everyone happy throughout the whole process – perhaps I had noticed that more than anyone – so I honestly think that to see the joy her wedding had created was the biggest treat that she had had all day.

It was a family full of love and laughter; they were all coming over, offering us drinks and kindness. We were treated with so much respect. It ended up being one of the happiest weddings I have ever attended.

It nearly wasn't but despite everything thrown in Sabrina's way, she had made it a success. That process of planning the wedding and getting to know her own mind was so invaluable for her as she headed towards marriage, and in the end it was a truly wonderful day.

The Bride Who Couldn't Decide: Sabrina

CHAPTER SIX

The Game-Changer

Delilah

She didn't want anything sparkly at all –
no crystals, no diamanté, no beads. This
was to be the first wedding dress I had
done without a single sparkle on it.

Some girls walk through my door and I instantly know there are dramas on the way. With others I don't know what I've got myself and my team into until we're cutting up the fabric. And then there are the girls who change the course of my business forever. One such girl was Shannon, who later appeared in my show, *Thelma's Gypsy Girls*. It was funny that she ended up in the factory with me, as it was her family who ordered the very first dresses with diamanté on them from me.

The Game-Changer: Delilah

Shannon's mum Margaret was one of my first customers, back when I still worked in Paddy's Market before Nico or the TV show. I was still doing exclusively kids' stuff, not weddings. Margaret would come in and buy stuff for Kathleen, her baby sister, and then her daughters Shannon and Shamelia. She would buy wonderful creations and always trusted me to let my imagination run free. Then one day she had a suggestion: she wanted a dress with some diamonds on it. She was the first person ever to ask for this. I had never done it before, but I looked into it and came up with something. That first dress for Shannon was for her to wear to a wedding. It had a full collar of diamonds, as well as cuffs of them at the ends of the sleeves and then some more scattered on the skirts like fairydust. It was beautiful, that little dress.

At that time I would never have thought that a few years later I would be working with Kathleen and Shannon on TV and I certainly had no idea that those sparkly dresses would be the future of my business. When I made the move to wedding dresses there was not a single gown I made that did not have some sort of diamanté, crystal or sparkle on it. That was until I met Delilah Purcell, when once again I was about to embark on a once-in-a-lifetime experience.

When Delilah first came to see me about her wedding I had already done loads of dresses for her family, the Purcells. I'd made bridesmaids' dresses for Delilah quite a few times in the past as well, so we knew and liked her. We had also done a wedding dress for her sister Sarah for an earlier

TV show before *My Big Fat Gypsy Wedding*, back in 2005. Sarah's dress was really something: it was backless and definitely the fanciest garment we had created at Nico at that time. Like all the girls I see, she wanted something a little bit different; for Sarah this meant actual crystals all over it.

Now these aren't like the usual gems we use, these are small three-dimensional beads with a tiny hole through the centre of each one so they are sewn onto the dress, not fixed with glue. They're made by Swarovski and are called Bicone Beads. They change colour in the light to create a truly magical effect. They are more expensive than the regular ones but you can tell when the dress is made up, especially if it's on a girl as gorgeous as Sarah.

Her bridesmaids were very different too. Instead of the usual pastels or pinks that a lot of the bridal parties go for, her bridesmaids were wearing red and black, all accesssorised with top hats.

The wedding took place in Scotland even though the family is not from there, and it was a great day. We went up and dressed Sarah, and we had a great relationship with that family. I loved the mother especially – she is a good, kind woman. She was really relaxed, we got on very well. There were six sisters; the eldest is Phyllis, who tends to do a lot of the talking for the younger girls, almost in a matriarchal role. She has never got married so she's taken on a bit of a mother-hen position – which is probably why the mother is so relaxed now! Sarah's wedding all went off without incident and I carried on making clothes for the family for the next few years. Then Delilah herself got engaged.

I was really happy for her when she came to the shop engaged. She too wanted something a bit different, but she had gone in a totally different direction to Sarah. Firstly, she wanted a dress that was pure silk, rather than

This was to be a seriously big challenge: six weeks to design and make a dress, with no input from the bride. There was only one thing to check.

'Have you changed your mind about the diamonds?'

'No,' she said. 'I definitely still want a silk dress but do you think everyone will talk about me if I don't have any Swarovski or anything? I don't want people to think we've got no money if I don't have them, cos it's not like we can't afford them – I just want something different.'

'Not at all, love!' I replied. The challenge was getting even bigger. 'I know that me and Leanne can come up with a design that will make the statement that you can afford a really special dress – there are other ways we can do this beyond crystals.

'We can cut it in new original ways, we can make it unusual; we can make you a totally unique dress. Trust us.'

Personal taste is one thing – and this girl has great taste – but what people say about you is also really important to travellers. She had spent a fortune on that silk, and she had already paid a lot of money for all the bridesmaids' dresses, so it was important that I could live up to the promises I was making.

Luckily, the dresses for the bridesmaids were not as complicated as they might have been. There were only four – and two of them were little ones. Their dresses really complemented our design for Delilah. They were ivory but very understated, with no diamonds, just like the bride's. Instead, they had huge Christmas flowers on them, which created a really dramatic effect. This glamorous entourage meant that the pressure for the main dress was really mounting.

But instead of feeling nervous I was starting to get excited – I was looking forward to the challenge. This was something we could really get our teeth into.

By the time I had finished talking to Delilah I couldn't wait to get on with it. It was a project where I'd really be able to stretch my wings and see what I could do. When Leanne and I sat down to plan we were like, 'Yes! Let's go for it! Let's just do this!'

We had all this fabric so we didn't have to persuade someone to buy it, or to go along with our ideas; we literally had a blank canvas and the chance to brainstorm. It was a once-in-a-career opportunity.

I bought a book on Dior, and another on Alexander McQueen too, as he had long been one of my favourite designers. We looked at all the silhouettes in the Dior book and then at the structures in the McQueen one – we also found a video of McQueen's last show online and we watched how the models moved. The pleats on a dress in the Dior book really caught my imagination: it was from the 1950 'Verticale' Line, working with pleats and bustles. The dress had a series of semi-circular pieces of pleated fabric layered on top of each other to create a sort of scalloped skirt. It was a real fairytale dress but not in the princessy way that most of my others are.

I showed it to Leanne: 'Look at that – it's amazing! Shall we try something like that?'

It was decided: we were going with the pleats. There was only one hurdle left – could we get it pleated in time? Because pleats aren't something you can just iron in yourself, you have to get them done by machine. It's a really specialist skill and not many places do it. Basically you have to make your dress (allowing the excess fabric that will make up the pleats), then take it apart again, then get the individual pieces

The Game-Changer: Delilah

pleated again and reconstruct the dress once you have got it all back.

I had done this a few times before, making First Communion dresses for little girls, but nothing on this scale. For years I'd been teaching myself how to do it by trial and error but this time I had no room for error.

If I just sent the fabric off to be pleated and hoped for the best, it would be a complete disaster when I began to make the pattern into a dress. So we had to design and make the dress fast, in order to leave time for it be sent away for pleating.

There were about 30 or even 50 pieces in this dress, with individual scallops forming the skirt and then fan details on both the waistline and neckline.

It was Leanne and me up late with cups of tea, and with our imaginations really going for it. She was the creative force, coming up with ideas for fans in certain places and ways to use the fabric and the girl's natural good looks as best as possible. 'If we put a fan on it here, we can adjust it to do that,' became her catchphrase for a few days! We were so excited to be let loose on such a different project.

Then came the time to cut the fabric. With every dress this is a big deal – it's the moment of no return. As I often

The Game-Changer: Delilah

do, I called Delilah again – she really hadn't bothered us at all: 'OK, are you 100 per cent sure? We have to cut into this silk today and it's going to look really silly with diamonds on it if you change your mind after the way we have designed it.'

But she was sure: 'No, I know that I don't want to be like all the others.'

There was a lot of trust here now: she knew she could trust us, she knew we wouldn't let her down, and we knew she was not a girl who would cause a fuss later or be difficult about money, or anything like that. Really, this was a relationship that could only have come about after years of working with the community, after knowing her family and seeing her sisters through their own weddings and so on.

She knew she was going to have an amazing dress and that we wouldn't be indiscreet. So when I ended the call I looked at Leanne, smiled and said: 'Let's do this!'

It got to the stage where only three weeks were left; the dress had been designed and 'made', now for the pleating. There are two pleating companies left in Britain and I had one in mind all the time we had been designing that I knew I wanted to send it to. I'd worked with them in the past and I knew we had a good relationship. I gave them a call to set up sending the materials to them but it turned out the owner, who I had always thought seemed really old, had retired suddenly and the factory had closed down. My heart was pounding – this girl's hopes and dreams depended on our plan and now it all hung on the one pleating company. This was a situation we had not accounted for.

We had to trawl the Internet in search of the other company who could do these pleats for us – the dress depended on it. Eventually we got hold of them and told them what we needed. They could do it. My breathing grew faster as I got to the million-dollar question: 'And how long is this going to take?' I winced, ready for the answer.

'Between four and six weeks.'
There was no way that would work for Delilah and now I knew I had to fight her corner.
'And, um, is there any room for manoeuvre with those timings?' I asked, my heart rate rising.
'Not really, love – we've got a lot of formalwear on at this time of year.'

'I understand, I really do, but I've got a girl here who's getting married in a few weeks and I've promised her a dream dress …'

The Game-Changer: Delilah

'You can't make promises like that about wedding days!' came the answer.

'I know, I know, but my usual pleater's closed down. I've been left high and dry, and this is a girl I'm really fond of. I'm friends with her family and she's come to me begging for a knock-out dress, fast.'

'Hold on, love, let me have a look at the schedule.'

I barely breathed for the minute and a half that the line was silent while he shuffled through papers on his desk.

Given they were one of the last pleating companies in the country, I didn't fancy my chances, but they were incredibly patient and after a bit more pleading and cajoling on my part, they finally agreed to do it. They really were amazing.

'OK,' he said. 'Get it down to us and we'll see what we can do – we will try our hardest.'

Packing the dress up to get it over to them was another adventure – there were just so many small pieces and it was fiddly. We knew it would be fantastic once it was all done but when it was in parts, it was a mess with bits here and bits there, tiny pieces of fabric all over. Obviously we were in a rush now as the company needed as much time as possible, but we had to make sure it was all packed up and properly labelled. One of us was packing while the other was working on labels and instructions – 'We need so many circles of this size, so many of these', and so on.

In the end, getting it packed took so long that I couldn't even give them two weeks to get the pleating all done. We had to allow for getting the dress back in pieces, with a good clean week to put the whole thing back together again, get it fitted on the girl and ready for the big day.

After ten days of Leanne and me gnawing our nails about the deadline, we got the pleats back; they were in an amazing condition and they were on deadline.

It felt as if through every stage of the process we were getting the best out of people, so we just knew that from now on in we must give it our best too.

For the next week Leanne and I were at the factory late every night, working on the dress. In the end I was working so late that I just stayed there. I slept in the factory for over a week.

We had a little two-seater sofa in there for family to sit on while watching the brides and I made it my own. I found an old quilt, brought in a couple of pairs of jogging bottoms and basically stayed in the same outfit, day and night, until it was done. I got the girls to bring me food when I needed it, and I was brushing my teeth and splashing my face in the basin in the toilet.

Constructing that dress with all its pleats was the biggest technical challenge I have ever faced, but I just knew I had to do it. When you get the pleats back to create fans, as we were doing on that dress, they are all in a selection of asymmetric circles.

It was so difficult to get them all attached to the dress properly and hanging right. These were weights and patterns I was unfamiliar with, and sewing the folded fabric of pleats was so tricky.

The dress was there on a mannequin in the corner of the factory and every now and then I'd need a break from it.

If I went to my office then had to go to the toilet, I'd have to walk past it – I'd got that tired and that stressed, I was sure it was looking at me! I'd go with my face covered so I couldn't see it there, taunting me. I didn't want to look at it, let alone have it looking at me, it had done my head in so, so much.

But I'd come out of the bathroom, see it and think, Actually, I know what we can do! The problem would dissolve and I'd soon be off again. That said, there were some long,

179
The Game-Changer: Delilah

lonely nights working with the thing and I'd be tweeting at dawn, desperate for a bit of company.

Honestly, I got to a point where I was screaming at it, just shrieking at this dress, wanting it all to fit together, but it was so fiddly. I felt like it was defeating me and all the while I was shouting at it: 'Why are you doing this? Why do you want to do this to me? What did I do to deserve this?'

So now and then I'd have to walk away from it and send a few messages to friends and family.

As the deadline got closer, I became increasingly aware that there were loads of people behind me, all willing me to find a way to get this dress together. The trouble was, the nicer they were, the more pressure I felt myself under!

It did help in the end, though. If it's four in the morning and you've been talking to pins and cloth all night, you just want a bit of human contact. Those tweets from people created an emotional reason to carry on; their encouragement showed me it how meant so much to so many people beyond Leanne, Delilah and me. It was the first time that I'd realised how much those dresses mean to people who will never see them. Of course I know every dress that I make means the world to the bride it is intended for, and to her immediate family,

but I hadn't realised how the attention from the show and from Twitter had meant that other people are now invested in those dresses. Even if they'll never get to wear one, folk like to know that the dream dress is always out there.

All those people have faith in me, I told myself. It's not a madness that I thought I could do something a bit different – I've got no faith in myself right now but someone else has.

In the end we cracked it, we really got on with it and we made it work. It was amazing! I had hated that dress more than I'd ever hated anything before but, once it was finished, I knew that it was worth every moment of stress. There was still one final test, though: Delilah herself.

She turned up with her sister and as I opened the door, I thought, Shit, she's going to be furious! But they walked in, took one look at the dress and burst into tears. That didn't help my nerves but I soon realised they were happy tears. 'It's absolutely amazing,' she gasped. 'I have never seen anything like it!'

Now this kid would have looked good in anything, she is absolutely stunning. No matter what you tried to do to her, she would have looked amazing but when she stepped out of the changing area, I knew this dress really was something.

I was terrified that it would look too plain without the crystals and she'd be disappointed, but she looked like nothing I had ever seen before. I couldn't go to the wedding because I had other commitments, but Leanne and Chelsea went to dress her.

They told me that on the day Delilah looked as incredible as we'd hoped. She opted not to wear a veil in the end. Instead she had her hair up and fresh flowers pinned in it.

She looked serene and glowing, as if she'd been born to wear that dress. I don't think I ever have, or ever will, see a girl as gorgeous wearing a dress I have been quite so proud of; it was the perfect match of me being so fond of her and so proud of the dress itself.

Everyone still talks about that dress, it will never be forgotten. No one has ever been quite brave enough to go for it again in that way, though.

People think choosing that dress means that they can't afford to have crystals, but the Nico team, Delilah and me all know what went into that dress and how special it was. There will never be another one like it, but the team and I will always know that we have it in us to do something like that.

I adored that girl, and I adored that dress.

CHAPTER SEVEN

The Family Rivalry

Maureen

I knew that we had to be absolutely loyal to the mother-of-the-bride in this wedding. We could not divulge the reasons for any of her decisions, nor any details of the order itself.

he travelling community is an incredibly tight-knit one, where everyone seems to know everyone else, and if not they know someone who is related to someone they know. Families are huge and sprawling as they marry young and have a lot of kids early on, meaning often there are quite a few generations around at the same time. And they are very respectful of family ties … most of the time. But sometimes, it can be murder. In any community weddings can be a real source of family aggravation and the travellers are no different.

The Family Rivalry: Maureen

I dread becoming involved in a family feud, but you can never get away from families in the wedding business and there are times when I'm involved before I've realised it.

Last year a woman from Bristol came into the shop as both her daughters were getting married that year and she wanted me to do both weddings. This often happens with the way that traveller families tend to have children close together and it can put a real strain on the family and their finances – the two biggest expenses of a man's life coming at the same time is not ideal.

This woman, Mrs MacDonagh, came in for an appointment, accompanied by her two daughters. They were all on time and the meeting went well from the offset. She was really upfront about the fact that with two weddings in one year, there would have to be a cap on what they could spend on them. They were also very specific that both girls had the same budget – there wasn't to be any funny business with one sister wise-cracking her way to more glitz and glamour than the other. I was briefed to keep an eye on the budgets throughout.

They ordered a wedding dress for each daughter and one outfit for the mother – the plan was that she would wear it to both ceremonies. And the dresses themselves were still to be as spectacular as any girl would have hoped. The mum's dress was ivory, trimmed in peach and mint-green silks. It was a slim-fitting, elegant dress, with a corset and a skirt with a wide fishtail bottom. We planned just to alter the skirts for the second wedding, later in the year.

The Family Rivalry: Maureen

The dress for the first wedding was inspired by none other than Bridal Barbie and we made as close to an exact replica as we dared. The fabric was glittering white, as opposed to Bridal Barbie's ivory, but the design was otherwise as close as we could get it.

There were huge netted skirts, dotted with tiny sparkling diamonds, and on top of them was an overlay of silk fabric, cut out in the same delicate swirling shapes as Barbie's.

Where the silk dipped and rose we added three 3D flowers – two at the front and one on the back – sewn onto the overlay and part of the swirling patterns. The bodice itself was classic Barbie too: white with three swirls of Swarovski crystals on either side.

What really made the dress stand out were the epaulettes on the shoulders. It was an unusual look for the dresses I usually make, but Bridal Barbie had them and so did this dress. They attached to the shoulder straps of the corset and had matching diamond swirls to echo the pattern on the skirts. Then, beneath the silk was a starburst of tulle with the same scattering of diamonds as the skirts. Like Barbie's, these were pretty serious epaulettes, coming at least a foot out from the bride's shoulders. You needed to have a fair

The Family Rivalry: Maureen

amount of confidence to wear the dress like this, but this girl had it in spades and we knew she would look great. The look was topped off with a short, almost perky-looking, veil, which suited the bride down to the ground.

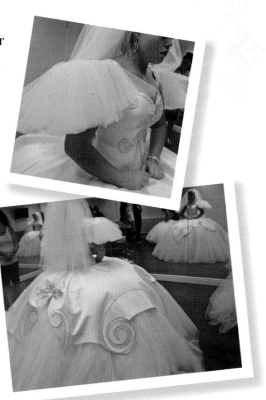

We were too busy at the time to take on the work of doing the bridesmaids' dresses too, but the mother really wanted us to make a mini-bride dress for the first wedding, which was due to take place in the August. That was no problem, especially as these are quite easy to design, being replicas of the wedding dress. I love doing these, and the mini Bridal Barbie was no exception. We decided on the same netted tulle skirts as her mentor, with the same sprinkling of diamonds but without the silk patterned overlay. She had a simpler corset, plain white with a few diamonds, and the same veil. My favourite part was that the little girl had matching epaulettes. As with the

The Family Rivalry: Maureen

skirt and corset, there was less detail but we didn't scrimp on size – they came out as far as the bride's!

We had a really lovely afternoon, putting all of these plans together, and I was looking forward to getting to grips with the designs we had come up with. I thought the mini-bride was going to be especially sweet and that the chosen little girl would be properly thrilled. When the family left Nico that day I had a huge grin on my face. It should have been the perfect order: charming people, reliable family and designs I knew we could do a good job on, but it's never that simple at Nico, I should have remembered that.

The next thing we knew, we had a phone call from the mother to say there were going to be two mini-brides. This really was quite unusual.

For starters, being a mini-bride is supposed to be a real mark of honour for the little girl who is chosen but also, who was the second mini-bride meant to be copying? Would she be a replica of a replica? For now, it seemed this was indeed the case. We didn't even know who the second mini-bride was going to be – the first was to be the bride's little sister, but the second remained a bit of a mystery. But the mum said she'd get the measurements for the second girl to us, and we told her we'd wait before cracking on with it. In the meantime, we had the bride's dress to be getting on with, so none of us were overly fussed by the situation.

A few weeks later – as is so often the case when wedding plans start changing – we had not heard back from her about

The Family Rivalry: Maureen

the plans for the second mini-bride. We left it another couple of weeks, just in case there was some kind of problem or illness behind the situation, but then Pauline and I decided to chase her up. Pauline gave her a ring to say that we really needed the measurements or we would not be able to start cutting out the fabric for the dresses. Again we were told that we'd get the measurements for the second mini-bride very soon, only for the promise to be followed by more silence.

In the end we got the measurements, but then we had a further call.

'Thelma, I need you to hold fire on that second mini-bride,' she said.
'What do you mean, babe?' I asked, confused.
'Just hold fire for now. It's been murder – all sorts of trouble going on.'

'Can I let you know at the end of the week? But don't start making it for now …'

I felt sympathetic towards what I thought was this woman's dilemma. She was a really nice woman, with a lovely manner and she hadn't ordered two outfits for herself for the weddings, despite being quite high-profile affairs in their community, but now she was having to stretch to two mini-bride dresses.

The Family Rivalry: Maureen

Not long after this decision we took a call from the groom's mother. This was almost unheard of in the circumstances and I think she only had the courage to call us because I had done a wedding for her daughter a few years before.

'My son is marrying this girl that you're making a wedding dress for,' she told me, all excited.

'Yes, love – she's a great girl and I love the designs we've come up with for her dress,' I said.

But she was none too keen to keep the informal chats going, this mother-in-law. 'Now, has she cancelled it?' she barked.

'Cancelled what?' I asked, the penny starting to drop.

'The second mini-bride,' she replied. 'It was my little girl who was supposed to be the second mini-bride and now there seems to be all sorts going on and I'm not having it!'

This is a situation you really need not to become involved in, a small voice in my head told me. Luckily, I managed to keep my thoughts to myself, and went for one of my fail-safe standby lines: 'I'm not sure about that, but I'll find out for you. I'll need to speak to Pauline and get back to you,' I added for good measure. 'I wasn't in the office that day.'

I don't know how many times a day I must say that about Pauline whenever I need to get out of something that comes up in the factory. Half the time I really do need to speak to Pauline – often she knows what's going on better than me – but if I'm totally honest, half the time it just means, 'I can't deal with having this conversation with you right now, I think something fishy might be going on.'

I never called the mother-of-the-groom back, but this did not seem to put her off in the slightest. She was determined to get to the bottom of what was going on with the double mini-bride situation and continued to call me time and again throughout the day.

Every ten minutes Pauline would be back in the office: 'It's her on the phone again, the same one – she really wants to know what's going on with the mini-bride set-up.'

'So do I!' came my reply. It was doing my head in, not knowing what was going on, but I knew we couldn't start giving away details of a wedding to extended guests, no matter how keen they might be for the info.

I'd learned this the hard way a couple of years ago. In the traveller community, often even close family members will do absolutely anything to find out details of a wedding before the big day itself. It's a big competitive game of one-upmanship and it can cause absolute mayhem with family relationships. They want to know about colours, styles or any kind of motif – I still don't really understand why, but I do know the whole thing can cause so much more grief than it's actually worth.

When we had the apprentices in the factory for *Thelma's Gypsy Girls*, we had to stop attaching names to any of the

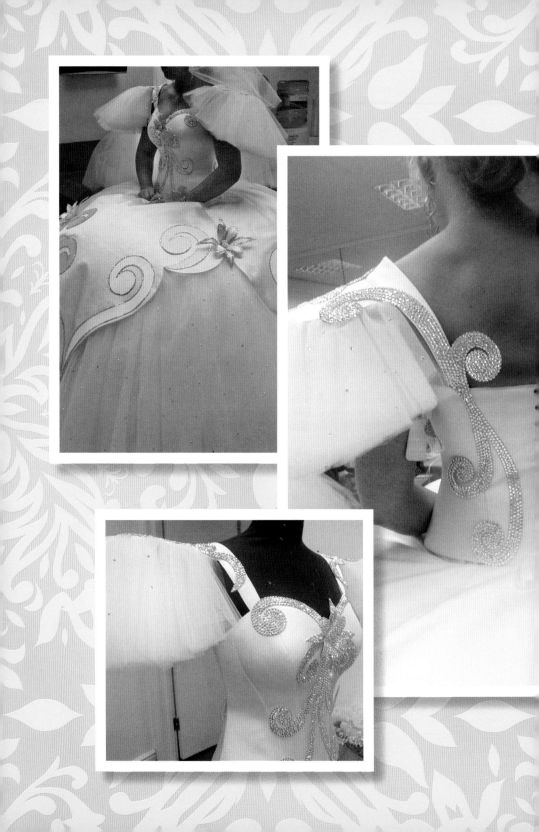

orders to prevent this kind of skullduggery.

Instead, we gave all our orders numbers and that was how we referred to them for the entire time that we had the travellers with us in the factory. Only Pauline and me knew which numbers corresponded to which names.

Even so, we almost got into trouble the minute that the traveller apprentice girls started work. Within days, one of the girls had spotted a selection of coloured bridesmaids' dresses on mannequins in the studio. We had not labelled or named them in any way, but nonetheless she walked up to them straight away, looked at me and said: 'These are for my cousins, aren't they?'

'Nah, they're just prom dresses,' I replied, with a bit of a brainwave. How on earth had she worked that out so fast, anyway?

'Yeah, they are,' said the girl, bold as brass.

The Family Rivalry: Maureen

This girl knew she could potentially cause chaos by divulging the details and we knew what a risk it was for the business ourselves, but in the end we got away with it.

Another time during the making of that show, we did a wedding where I wanted to invite two of the apprentices along as my assistants. This was a big deal because of the issues with secrecy that the travellers have. A lot of the brides that I approached just didn't want to have traveller girls that they didn't know to have any information about their dresses, even if they could not have told anyone of any significance. There was also the significant risk of some of the local boys trying it on with them.

'We can't have one of our lads grabbing either of those two,' was the response from one bride. 'There'll be murder, trying to sort something like that out.'

And she was probably right, that bride. There were also a couple of traveller girls that the bride said she definitely did not want coming to the wedding to help me. It was all too complicated to take the risk so we ended up taking two of the other girls instead.

Because of experiences like these, I knew that we had to be absolutely loyal to the mother-of-the-bride in this wedding. We could not divulge the reasons for any of her decisions, nor any details of the order itself. Even though we knew the mother-of-the-groom and had had a good relationship with her in the past, the fact remained that this time it was not her order, so she was not owed the same loyalty. Nevertheless, we had to find out what was going on – if only to stop me from putting my foot in it by mistake.

Eventually, after a rather delicate phone call, it was established that the mother-of-the-groom had requested the second mini-bride, in what seemed to be an attempt to be a bit more involved in the wedding. It's unusual for the groom's family to get this involved, so it did seem like a slightly odd set-up. I'm still not entirely sure if that was actually the case, but it seemed like it. Consequently – and understandably, I thought – the mother-of-the-bride had said that she had not budgeted for two mini-brides and so she asked the groom's family to pay. This had not been met with a great response, and it was what had landed us with The Great Mini-Bride Standoff we were now all dealing with.

Meanwhile, the mother-of-the-groom continued to call and eventually the number of unanswered calls that we had from her on one day reached 57.

We were desperate to stay out of the situation, but when it reached that level we had to at least try and have a diplomatic

The Family Rivalry: Maureen

conversation. It turned out that what she now wanted was to have a mini-bride at the wedding with her own design: if the bride's family could not, or would not, supply a second dress, she would do it herself. I don't know if it was, but it was starting to look a lot as if the mini-brides were in competition!

'We don't want to talk to you about it,' I tried to explain to her. 'It's not personal but it's not you behind this wedding, and so our loyalties can't lie with you this time.'

'You know me, you've done a wedding for me,' she pleaded with me.

'Absolutely, love. And you know I'm dead fond of you. We'll do you a gorgeous dress for the little girl,' I offered, 'but we can't do a mini-bride that doesn't match the bride – it's just not right.'

'Oh come on, Thelma,' she said, still pressing and continuing to go on about her plans.

We called the mother-of-the-bride again and explained that we couldn't hold off the groom's mother any more. We could tell the poor woman did not want a feud of any sort but she was worried and what could she do? And so we agreed to keep the slot open for her.

A couple of hours later the grooms's mother called back: 'We're cancelling it,' she decisively announced.

'*You're* cancelling this kid's dress? You're sure?' I said.

The Family Rivalry: Maureen

'Yes, yes, I am! You phone her and tell her,' she replied.

'No, you phone her and tell her – you're the one making this decision.'

I had to be firm with her, but in the end I obviously wasn't firm enough as it ended up being me calling the mother-of-the-bride to say there wasn't going to be a second mini-bride. All the while, the groom's mother tried to persuade us to make a different dress for her little girl.

'I'll pay for it,' she said. 'I'll pay anything!' She really did want that little girl to have a mini-bride dress.

'No,' said Pauline, who had been drafted in to take over the call. 'This just feels too much like one-upmanship, which we don't want to get involved in – we just can't. It's not personal, we know you just want that little girl looking an absolute cracker – and we totally understand that. But it's a fair business decision we have to take.'

In the end we said, we will do you a dress in any colour that you choose, but we will not do a white dress – we simply won't do a dress for the little one that is in any way similar to the bride's.

When August came around, the wedding went ahead with the second mini-bride there. Despite everything we had tried to do to keep out of the brewing inter-family competitiveness, the mother-of-the-groom had gone ahead and got the little girl a mini-bride's outfit elsewhere.

I was devastated when I heard, and I can only imagine the family's faces when they saw that kid turn up at the church in a white dress.

I really felt for the original mini-bride, who had been so excited the day that she came to pick up her outfit. I'll never forget her face when she saw what she'd be wearing – she was grinning from ear to ear all morning. Luckily – for her and me – everyone at the wedding knew it wasn't me who had been disloyal, as apparently the dress the second mini-bride had was clearly of inferior quality. Travellers can spot a Nico dress a mile off, thank God!

The Family Rivalry: Maureen

CHAPTER EIGHT

The Bumpy Road to the Altar

'No, love, it's not early pregnancy,' she
replied. 'She's due in three weeks.'
I was genuinely gobsmacked. No wonder
we had all noticed – she was eight months
pregnant with twins!

Time and again I find myself reminded that one of the reasons why I work so much with the traveller community is because they know that they can count on my discretion: about money, the surprise of the dress itself, and about the date and venue of the wedding. Oh, and there's one other thing too … From time to time a girl comes along with a problem that can't be hidden with discretion, this particular difficulty needs a few physical amendments to the dress as well.

The Bumpy Road to the Altar

Yes, despite their very strict upbringing and the huge value that they place on the idea of girls keeping their honour intact, every now and again I see a bride who is undeniably pregnant. Well, I say undeniably, but some try and deny it anyway, despite what is staring us all in the face.

One of the most extraordinary examples came a couple of years ago when an otherwise totally normal-seeming girl came in and knocked the whole team for six. Talk about a learning curve! The young bride-to-be – who shall remain nameless – came into our old factory with her sister and ordered a wedding dress. Chatty and confident, she was a typical traveller girl. We were not quite so established as a company then – we were big in the traveller community but not famous, so customers could just walk in off the street and still be seen. These days an appointment is essential.

Back then we could make the dresses much more quickly. Now we have to take an order and then it can take a few months for us to have space in the schedule so the girls have to order well in advance. But in those days we could get on the case much faster. This dress was ordered about six months before the wedding, though, as the family was going travelling for a while. But then the bride-to-be came back to me only a little while later and said that she needed the dress quicker because the boy was in trouble and might be getting locked up. It wasn't the first time that I'd heard something like this – I hadn't been working with the travellers for too long, but I'd already learnt a lot – so this didn't phase me in the slightest.

The Bumpy Road to the Altar

The dress was made as fast as we could manage and the girl came in to try it on and collect it, as is usual. She had what seemed like the entire family with her this time: her sister, her mother and her sister-in-law, not to mention a handful of bridesmaids and countless other little siblings, who made themselves at home in the factory, running around and causing mayhem. It was winter and the girl had a thick polo-neck jumper on. As this was in the old factory, we did not have a lovely changing room and big 'reveal room', unlike the facilities we have now. The girls just had to get changed right there and this one was no different.

We were all chatting excitedly, as is often the way. With that many women in one small area, the volume sometimes gets pretty intense and we also get excited to see our creations on the girls, so we don't really mind these moments of intensity. I am surprised that despite all that din no one heard my jaw hit the floor when the girl took her jumper off, though.

This was not the hint of a bump. This was not the confusing roundness of a girl who might have been indulging over the winter or might be four months pregnant.

This was not a suggestion, exaggerated in the light.

This was a huge bump!

It wasn't even a new bump; it was already quite low. The curve of her pregnant belly went from right down the top of her pelvis all the way up to beneath her boobs. She was undeniably, and quite heavily, pregnant – I was guessing at six months. But that wasn't even the extraordinary thing: the real surprise was that everyone in the room was ignoring it.

The Bumpy Road to the Altar

I looked around at the faces of the other women in there. They were all chatting or staring about, looking at pieces of fabric or other designs in the room. Not one of them was looking at this girl, or her bump.

I stared around her to Pauline, who was behind her, ready to try and fasten the dress's corset. Pauline was staring right back, her eyes round – even from behind, it was perfectly clear that this girl was in at least her second trimester.

'So, this corset then …' I said, wincing at Pauline.
It's going to kill her … or the baby, I was thinking to myself.

I tried to make a face at Pauline that somehow managed to say, 'Please don't pull it too tight!'

I was genuinely worried about the girl. Then, just at that moment, Leanne came into the room with an accessory that I'd asked her to bring. She was in full chatterbox mode herself, but as she turned into the room her nattering stopped dead and her eyes widened.

'Here you go, love – is this what you were after? Whoa!'

I turned around and glared at her, hoping and praying, even if it was blindingly obvious, she didn't say anything until one of the family did.

I watched as her smile froze into a polite mask and she looked with panic at her mum Pauline and then at me. She

could not have appeared more obvious if she'd had 'What do I say?' tattooed on her face. We just glared back and hoped for the best.

Meanwhile, everyone else carried on chattering without a care in the world. It was a mystery whether they had not noticed, or if they were in complete denial, hoping we wouldn't.

'So then, this corset …' I said, trying to bring a bit of focus to the room.

I carefully lifted it and held it against her front – all of it – handing the straps at the back to Pauline. She nodded, seeming to understand the situation.

As Pauline pulled the corset against the girl's body, one of the sisters chipped in: 'Hey, it looks as if she's put on a bit of weight – doesn't it, Thelma? You're really going to have to pull on that corset, Pauline!'

With that she started giggling, as did the rest of the family. The girl herself smiled serenely and it remained a mystery as to exactly who in that room actually knew what was going on.

After some delicate tugging and balancing, we eventually had to tell the poor bride that we would need to insert a modesty piece at the back of the corset.

We were desperate not to make her feel uncomfortable as we weren't even sure whether she knew if her family knew, if indeed she herself had realised what was going on.

'I must have got in a bit of a muddle,' I found myself saying. 'What we need to do is add a piece of fabric at the back, behind where these laces will go across your back – we call it a "modesty piece". That way all the skin will be covered and you'll have a lovely smooth line.'

Pauline was nodding and agreeing frantically with everything I said. We didn't think we could tell the girl that our measurements indicated she needed a 12-inch modesty piece. And that was in addition to the five inches we noticed we'd need to take the skirts out. I was terrified of hurting her, but I was just as worried about landing her in it with her family. By the time the lot of them left, Pauline and I were nervous wrecks.

As soon as the factory door closed, we all just looked at each other, totally aghast.

'Were we the only ones that saw that?' asked Leanne, giggles erupting from her.

'Do they honestly not realise what's going on, or was that some kind of a wind-up?' said Pauline, the bemusement still visible on her face.

'I don't know – were they in denial? Were they ashamed in front of us, or do they genuinely not realise?' I asked. I was as mystified as anyone else in the office.

'That was one hell of a confusing situation!' said Leanne, shaking her head. 'When I came in, I didn't know if it was rude not to congratulate the girl or if it would have been the worst thing in the world – my mouth was just hanging open.'

'Yeah, we noticed!' said Pauline, finally letting the lighter side of the situation out of her.

'But they didn't seem shocked, and they didn't seem to care about covering it up either. They just–'

' … carried on talking as if nothing remotely interesting was happening at all!'

'Why was she so unselfconscious about the bump and yet so unprepared to admit it was there? What were we supposed to say?'

We carried on wondering about that situation for the rest of the week in the office – it became a bit of a water-cooler classic.

The following Monday a cousin of the girl, with whom I was working on another wedding, called the office.

'I'm not being funny, dear,' I said to her, once I'd plucked up the guts, 'but that girl, your cousin, she's pregnant – isn't she?'

'Yeah, she's having twins,' came the reply.

'Oh my God, I thought she was quite big for only being gone a few months!' I said, rather pleased with my detective skills.

'No, love, it's not early pregnancy,' she replied. 'She's due in three weeks.'

I was genuinely gobsmacked. No wonder we had all noticed – she was eight months pregnant with twins! And the next time we heard from that cousin, it turned out she had given birth a fortnight after the wedding. For weeks I would find myself still amazed at how that family had behaved in the name of honour. Surely they knew? But then again, sometimes I wonder. Just when you think you've seen it all …

What amazes me most about this story is that it isn't even the most dramatic pregnancy that we have had to deal with at Nico, as Leanne reminded me recently. In the early years of us working with travellers on their wedding dresses we had a girl come in and order the most stunning lace creation. It really was an original piece: a corset top with a big butterfly on it and the whole thing was made of lace. It had a 25-foot lace trail as well. For me, it was a real one-off, up there with Delilah and her pleated dress – a challenge and a treat to work on. And they were a lovely family, too: they kept their appointments, they paid their deposit on time and they were no fuss and always a pleasure to talk to. They really were the whole package.

In those days the company wasn't as big as it is now, and we didn't have the facilities or the staff that we do today. We used to have to send off to Israel to get the basis for the wedding corsets made; they would come back and then we would decorate them. So we measured this girl for her corset and sent off the order as that part was to be standard despite the unusual lace of the rest of the dress.

A couple of months later she came back to the factory with her mum and two sisters to try it on. I was really busy and had foreseen no problems at all with the order, so I got her trying things on without delay. She was a pretty sturdy girl anyway – not fat, but strong-looking. And this was January, so we were all in pretty chunky jumpers – she was no different. But when we got the corset on her, it was instantly apparent that it was way too small.

There were handfuls of her boobs spilling out over the top, and it simply didn't go round at the back; it was more than several inches too narrow.

I was pretty distracted at this point, and I hadn't really had a chance to look at her without her top on. As a result, my

The Bumpy Road to the Altar

immediate assumption was that I had made a mistake with the measurements. I was mortified – this wasn't a situation as with Chloe and her skirts, I couldn't just whip something up quickly in its place; this corset had been specifically ordered from abroad. And the whole mess was totally my responsibility.

Pretty quickly, we realised that we would have to do a massive modesty piece on the back. I called Pauline in to help me with taking the measurements. I had the tape measure around her again and said – still totally assuming that I was in the wrong:

'Bloody hell, love! What have you been eating? A lot of pies this Christmas?'

And then I looked up and saw her face. In that instant I realised how badly I had just put my foot in it.

Me and my big mouth twittering on, and there she was, filled with dread.

She was staring at me with these big eyes, as if to say, 'Please, please, please don't keep talking! I would give anything for you to stop talking now.'

Oh hang on, I thought to myself, we've got a bit of a situation here.

'Stupid me, I must have gone and ordered the wrong size!' I said, trying to avoid eye contact with anyone at all by this

The Bumpy Road to the Altar

point. 'I think this is my fault, so I'll put a good piece on the back.'

And with that I tried to get on with the rest of the appointment as breezily and quickly as I possibly could.

As I learned later with the bride who was eight months pregnant with twins, while travellers don't mind admitting after the wedding that there may have been a little, shall we say, 'discrepancy with the dates', it's a really big deal for them to admit to anything on the day itself or beforehand, even if it's impossible not to notice. Because of this I was terribly worried that I might have landed the girl in trouble. As it was, they paid for the rest of the dress and were due to come in the following week to pick it up with its few amendments.

It was the Saturday morning when the mother appeared at the shop door. I was in, catching up on a bit of paperwork, when she knocked on the door.

'Oh hello, love,' I said only for her to burst into floods of tears.

It was two days before the wedding. Knowing what I did, I assumed the news would not be good, but realised I could not preempt it. After a minute or two she was in proper floods of tears, just sobbing – I couldn't get a word out of her.

All of the dress's components were there, packed up and ready to go. We'd worked hard on them and it was every bit as fabulous as the original design had been.

Is it something we've done? I thought to myself. Is it something one of us said?

'What's the matter, love?' I asked in a nervous whisper, trying to calm her down. I put out a hand to stroke her back in a calming gesture.

'The wedding's off!' she announced suddenly, before a fresh burst of sobs unleashed themselves.

'What do you mean, how come?' I asked, just hoping the girl was OK.

'Well, it's been murder back at home, love,' she said through her tears. 'You won't believe it!'

'Oh no, you poor thing! Come and have a cup of tea.' I held the door open for her, ready to sit her down and talk through what we could do.

'So, can we have our money back on the dress?' asked the mum, her tone suddenly changing.

'Um, no, you've ordered it and we've done it. We had to ship in that lace especially for you. You know there's no way we can do that. Come and have a sit down, I'm sure it'll be OK and we can work something out.'

But then the girl's dad appeared at the door behind her. He looked exhausted and was clearly furious.

'This dress is no good to us now,' he said. 'The wedding's off!'

'But how was I to know that?' I replied. 'I've done what I was asked to – it's not my fault.'

'I'm f***ing telling you, we don't want that dress!' he roared at me.

'You'll never do any business again if you try and cross me or my family at this time. You don't know who I know and I'm not in the mood to be crossed on this!'

The trouble was, neither was I.

'Do you know what, I really don't care!' I said, my voice remaining calm and trying to stay dignified. 'The dress is there, ready. I have done my part of the bargain – you can come and get it or not.'

'What am I to do with it?' he said. 'Where am I even going to keep it?'

'Well, if you want me to store it until the wedding's back on, or until your daughter makes other arrangements, I will do. I've done it before and it's no problem for me. But I've made it for you, so I can't just give you your money back.'

At this point the mum was trying to step in and calm things down: 'Come on, let's not all get agitated …'

'I'm not agitated,' I replied. I was trying to make things as clear and simple as possible. 'Look, the dress is there. You come and get it when you want to.'

We left it at that.

The dress was so gorgeous that it would have broken all of our hearts not to use it.

It proved impossible to sell because travellers are so superstitious that no one was going to buy a wedding gown associated with scandal.

I am happy to say that we found a good home for it in the end, though, when the girl decided to have it made into two First Communion dresses for her younger relatives. That lace was absolutely stunning so even though I ended up having to keep it for more than a year, it was a joy to see that it ended up with a new life after all. It was the bride-to-be's nieces who got the finished dresses and they were beautiful little lacy creations − very delicate, with lots of gorgeous details, not the flamboyant styles that a lot of travellers have. And all of us at Nico were just happy that the dress went to a good home.

You see, sometimes it's not just the brides who create new life, sometimes it's the dresses themselves.

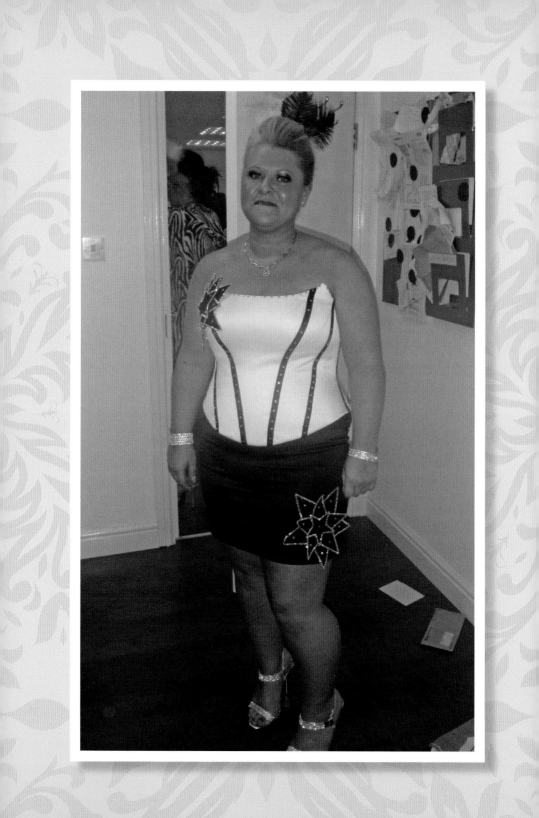

CHAPTER NINE

The Bride
Without a Wedding

Samantha

She had put her life on hold to become a
mother to her siblings and in doing so she
put paid to her own chances of becoming
a bride and a mother herself.

*I*t's always a bit of a scandal when a pregnant bride gets married but usually they do at least go through with the wedding. For a few traveller women, there is no wedding. And in a society where you are raised from day one to be a bride, this can be harsh, to say the least. Every now and again I come across one of these women – usually helping out a younger sister or cousin with their wedding – and my heart goes out to them. It's not the same as it is for non-traveller women, where there is a world of work and passion and choice.

The Bride Without a Wedding: Samantha

More often than not these women are tied to childcare and domestic chores – a set-up which makes it very hard to find love, or at least a husband, when you are considered 'past your best'.

In the past I have made the mistake of writing these women off, just as the rest of their society does. A few years ago we had a Rathkeale girl come in with her older cousin to order a wedding dress. She was only about 16, but the cousin was closer to 30. In Rathkeale the tradition is that while the girls get married at the youngest age of the spectrum – only about 16 or 17 – the blokes don't tend to do so until they're around 30. They prioritise making their way in business first, and marry later. When these girls came in, I immediately assumed the dress was to be for the younger girl as the older girl was way past traditional Rathkeale marrying age. I was right, and we focused on the younger kid for the entire appointment. But then the older one, who had seemed a bit of a live wire throughout, took me to one side shortly before they left.

'Thelma, Thelma!' she whispered.

'Yes, love,' I replied.

'Now, you have to swear to tell no one …'

'OK, love,' I said.

'I'm getting married too,' she told me.

I seriously doubted this. Not only was she at least ten years older than the age at which girls get married in Rathkeale but she had also been behaving quite strangely all morning. And now the secrecy – what was all this about?

The Bride Without a Wedding: Samantha

'OK, love, great,' I replied.

She pulled me closer to her. 'And I want you to put that corset aside for me,' she said, pointing at one of the already made-up garments we had in the factory.

'I'm sorry, but I can't put things aside for you unless you've come in and made up a design and paid a deposit,' I said, convinced she was winding me up now.

'But it's me! You know it's me! I'm here now. I swear I'm coming back …'

There was a real sense of urgency in her whisper now.

'Honestly, love, I would if I could but if I start bending the rules for one girl then it just gets too chaotic.'

The situation was getting a bit awkward. She had never mentioned that she was even engaged before now and suddenly she was trying to extract promises from me about her future wedding dress. It all seemed a bit fishy.

'Please, Thelma, please!'

Anything for a quiet life! 'Alright, I'll put this one aside for a couple of weeks until you come back,' I told her.

But I had no real intention of doing so as I had made the assumption that she was, if not jealous, then at least slightly in awe of all the attention her younger cousin was getting and

The Bride Without a Wedding: Samantha

she just fancied a bit of the action herself.

To my shame, I don't think I even remembered to tell Pauline about her, and I certainly never put the corset aside. But I learned my lesson when the girl rang up a few weeks later to make an appointment for herself. I still didn't really believe her, as she was insisting on my utmost secrecy, but sure enough before long she turned up on time and ordered a magnificent dress.

Right up until the day she came to collect it there was a part of me that didn't believe this was ever going to happen but now I feel dead guilty that I let myself think that way. In hindsight, maybe her insistence on all the secrecy was because she felt the same way – perhaps she simply could not believe her luck. She ended up looking great in her dress, though – and my lesson was well and truly learned!

Since then I have changed my tune. These days, whenever I meet the older girls I usually find I like them – I admire their grit and their ability to hold on to a dream while getting on with life. About five or six years ago we had two girls come into Nico who were planning a double wedding. They were really excited to be sharing everything as they were friends, and

The Bride Without a Wedding: Samantha

one girl was marrying the other girl's brother. There was a lot of chatter and giggling the day they arrived. They were only 16, but had clearly been planning things for a while as they were brimming with ideas and sketches and little snippets of fabric.

From the word go we could see it would be quite a big order. The girls were having matching dresses and eight bridesmaids between them – some belonging to each girl, others shared.

The dresses themselves had strapless corsets with transparent lace panels in them, a delicate beaded halterneck and the traditional huge skirts, sprinkled with sparkling diamonds. Then, in a touch that I absolutely loved, we made each a lavish winter cape as it was a December wedding. We took the shape of those old Scottish Widows advertisements as our starting point for the inspiration but made them in white velvet, with a huge fur lining to the collar. So dramatic – they could have drowned the girls but they didn't, they just kept them warm while emphasising the delicate femininity of the dresses beneath. Like I said, this was not a wedding where anyone was doing things by halves.

The Bride Without a Wedding: Samantha

At first we weren't quite sure of the dynamic between the two families. One girl clearly had affluent parents, who were waving a hand at all costs. They wanted her to have whatever she wanted – money was no object and so they were giving her a free rein with the design and the budget. But Barbara, the second of the two brides, turned out to have been brought in not by her mother but by her elder sister, Margaret.

We found out their parents had died a while back and Margaret had ended up bringing up all of her younger siblings single-handedly ever since.

She was basically their mother, in every way but biologically; she was doing everything for them and had been for years. I took my hat off to her.

This woman had put her own life and dreams of a wedding on hold so that her siblings could have the very best chance in life. When I realised this I had a word with Pauline and the rest of the team and we made a note to be as discreet and respectful as we possibly could – we didn't want her to feel bad about trying to keep up with paying her half of the double wedding when the other half, the considerably better-off half, were so relaxed about costs. But she surprised us all: she had been saving for this eventuality for some time, and was determined to keep up. The grit and steeliness of this woman really was something else.

The Bride Without a Wedding: Samantha

For years and years she had slaved looking after those kids, saved everything she could, and with a quiet dignity she managed to keep up with everything that the other family paid for, matching it penny for penny, so that the day itself was as magical as she herself would have once hoped for.

For a while I felt dead sad for Margaret and I thought about her a lot after the weddings were finished. Sometimes I surprise myself with how much these stories touch me – I suppose it's because I myself have had hard times, being alone and let down, and I've grafted my way out of a bad place.

But it turned out I need not have worried that much as a few years later this women showed up again. She was about 28 now … and engaged! I was thrilled for her – her siblings had all grown up and gone their own way, and she herself had a second chance at life.

It seems mad that she was considered old and potentially over the hill at that age, but that's really how it is with the traveller community.

But now she was in love and planning her own wedding, and she wanted us to do her dress!

I was thrilled to be asked and we really did our best to do her proud. She chose a dress with a sort of sunburst motif, which really suited her sunny personality, especially now that

The Bride Without a Wedding: Samantha

she was in love. The skirts were not as massive as those we've done for some girls in the past; instead it was tier upon tier of silk ruffles, all piled up, each above the next. Each of the ruffles had a sprinkling of Swarovski crystals and on both the skirt and the bodice there was a dramatic sunflower design, with tiny strands of diamonds shooting from the edges.

She had a corset with discreet straps and loads of crystals on the corset design, trimming all of the edges and in shooting stripes across her body. To top it all off she had a veil and a stunning headpiece. It was a proper princessy tiara, and I was so proud of her that despite being a bride who was older than the norm, she didn't try and hide her light under a bushel – she really went for it, with a huge grin and a look of pride in her smile that went from ear to ear! We were made up to see such a happy ending for someone who had sacrificed so much for others, done such a good job and truly deserved a real shot at happiness herself. I still feel good about her whenever I think back.

And I've been thinking about Margaret a lot recently because just a few months ago, I met another girl who inspired me in a similar way. This girl didn't come in with family for a wedding: she was part of the Channel 4 show, *Thelma's Gypsy Girls*. I loved doing that show, I really did – but I was really not prepared for what an ordeal it would be!

In the past when I've dealt with the traveller community I have been in a position to command their respect – usually they want a dress so they want my full attention.

The Bride Without a Wedding: Samantha

They need my input to make the whole outfit as good as it can possibly be. But with *Thelma's Gypsy Girls* this was far from the case. I took on a selection of traveller girls from all different parts of the community (originally ten) and decided to give them a few months' training in dressmaking skills.

It wasn't just about the dressmaking, though – I really wanted these girls to experience a snippet of the confidence and sense of achievement that working had given me.

I wanted to show them they could do more than domestic work and planning weddings, that they would always have options with a little bit of education. It was more than sewing skills that I wanted these girls to go away with, but I think it was me who learned the most from that experience.

I had not realised how young these girls would seem as a result of their lack of formal schooling. We had to get a tutor in to teach them the basics of telling the time, as well as literacy skills. And many of the girls just wanted to mess around – they were well into their teens but would behave like 11-year-olds. Amidst all the chaos and drama there was one girl who really stood out: Samantha.

Samantha didn't appear in the Channel 4 show that much as generally she just kept her head down and got on with the

The Bride Without a Wedding: Samantha

work in hand. There were no shrieks or fights, no calls from parents or from the police about this one. Samantha was 34 when I first met her; we came across her as a result of my request for apprentices on Facebook. Her initial application was really good and she seemed keen to learn. She was from St Helens and I went up there to see her and we got on very well. I had an almost immediate respect for her when she explained everything she had to do at home. Her mum had died when she was very young and after that her dad had just left. As a teenager this left her all alone, with the sole responsibility of bringing up three young boys, her younger brothers.

She had put her life on hold to become a mother to her siblings, and in so doing she put paid to her own chances of becoming a bride and a mother herself.

For non-travellers, 34 might be considered the peak of your professional life, or a personal high point when you embark on a family after a couple of years of marriage, but it was all very different for Samantha.

Thirty-four means something quite different in the traveller community. Many travellers would say her life was nearly over by this point.

Of all the girls that I took on for the show, Sam was the most committed to getting a real education and a future

The Bride Without a Wedding: Samantha

out of it. The others had a good time and had some ideas and options opened up for them, but for Samantha it was a real lifeline. On top of that, it offered a chance for her to realise a dream that she'd started to believe she would never be able to follow.

A few weeks into the course, after a huge amount of drama and complications from what seemed like every corner of the factory, I began to realise that giving the girls a little fun and silliness now and again allowed them to get a bit of energy out of their systems and also meant they'd concentrate better afterwards, as well as showing them that I trusted them and wanted the best for them. So one day, when a couple of the ringleaders requested they be able to try on some of the dresses in the factory, I gave in and said yes. After all, if there was one thing those apprentices had taught me it was that if you keep putting your foot down, they just rebel more.

'Why not?' I told Leanne and Pauline. 'If we give them a little bit, they'll give a bit back.'

The girls went wild with excitement, choosing the dresses that they each wanted to be wearing and which ones would wear which dresses.

The Bride Without a Wedding: Samantha

All of a sudden the whole place was a riot of colour as if our little factory in Liverpool had become a menagerie for a flock of birds of paradise. They all grabbed at the outfits they wanted to try on ... it was almost as if they'd been eyeing them up a while. Huge hooped skirts were battling other hooped skirts of different colours; some were in veils perched on top of their heads while others just grabbed at a bit of neon lace, plonked it on and hoped for the best!

'I feel like a princess!' cried one of the girls, and I smiled to myself, thinking about all those Disney and Barbie images that are so often handed to me. Feeling like a princess really is the heart of my business.

The girls carried on hugging each other, pretending to give each other rings, acting out bits of the wedding ceremony as if they were born to do it – which, after all, they are! But none of them were wearing real wedding dresses; they're just

233

The Bride Without a Wedding: Samantha

too precious to let these teenagers into. Instead they were all in prom dresses or bridesmaids' dresses from the shop. We'd allowed them to take their pick of the oranges, pinks and lime greens, with Flamenco skirts and acres of tulle and netting. And they were having an absolute riot, prancing all over the factory.

The place was awash with shrieks of laughter and colour. At one point one of the girls tried to vanish into the break room and all I could see was a river of bright frills cascading out of the room.

It was meant for cups of tea and flicking through the gossip magazines that room, not several bolts' worth of my fabric moving at speed!

And amidst it all Samantha stood there, smiling at the madness. I knew what she really wanted was to try on one of the wedding dresses but I also knew that I couldn't allow her to try on something that was being made specifically for someone else rather than the standard prom dresses the others were in. I wanted to give her a moment of reassurance, though – to let her know that it wasn't the be-all and end-all.

'You've got an awful lot closer to these dresses than a lot of girls do,' I said to her, giving her arm a stroke.

'I know, Thelma, and thank you,' she replied.

The Bride Without a Wedding: Samantha

'And you've got a skill now – something that won't let you down. You can't ever rely on a man 100 per cent,' I explained, 'but of all the other girls, you're the one who will really leave here able to do something for yourself.'

While we had that chat the other girls carried on clapping and cheering, causing mayhem with their pretend ring ceremonies and walking down the aisle. But I saw a couple of them – still young enough to assume their time would come – steal a glance at us, and probably realise what we were discussing. There was a feeling in the factory that they all understood what Samantha had been through in sacrificing her time for her brothers and they supported her desire to have her moment as the ultimate princess. While there had been a lot of bad blood and plenty of cat fights during their apprenticeships, Samantha had kept out of it all and was

The Bride Without a Wedding: Samantha

well-liked. There was genuine warmth towards her, that day especially.

A few days later when we were doing interviews with the girls to try and establish who we should give a place to, I asked each of them what they'd like to be doing in five years' time. While I was surprised that most of them seemed more career-minded than I could ever have hoped for, it was Samantha's answer that most surprised me most.

'Don't laugh at me,' she started, 'but I'd like to open my own shop.'

There was no way that I would ever have laughed at that response, especially from Samantha. In fact, it was the opposite – I nearly burst with pride.

I've seen so many brides come and go, and I know that for a lot of them married life is not all it was cracked up to be, so expanding these girls' horizons and providing someone like Samantha with an alternative future was for me a real dream come true.

With her there was a real sense that this was her second chance at making something of herself. The others were keen to have fresh perspective but ultimately I think they

The Bride Without a Wedding: Samantha

all believed they were heading to the altar as well. But with Samantha I like to think that I showed her there's more than one way in which a wedding dress can make you a better future.

Sure, it's nice to look great in one, but for me wedding dresses mean so much more than that.

I wore a simple lace dress when I got married – no long train, no fancy bodice – but making dresses for these traveller girls has provided me with a life that, in my darkest hours, I could never have dreamed of.

That life lasted, even when my marriage didn't, and I am happier now than I was on my wedding day. I just hope that I taught Samantha enough to create similar opportunities for herself.

The Bride Without a Wedding: Samantha

CHAPTER TEN

Me and My Big Mouth

Patricia

By the Thursday I had done everything
and asked everyone. There wasn't
a single person I hadn't called for
help. The situation was about to get
out of control.

The travellers have such a huge culture of secrecy that they rely on me not to disclose any details about the dress to other customers before the big day. I absolutely won't mention colours, shapes or themes – and definitely not money! In turn I myself have developed quite a radar when it comes to learning who to trust. Some people are keen to haggle with me for days but will then pay up immediately once a price is decided, whereas others pour everything they've got into a wedding and can only pay in installments.

Me and My Big Mouth: Patricia

I try to help wherever I can, which means the trust gets built even further. I could just fold, or not get around to making their dress on time. I could come up with something they didn't order, with a smile and a breezy, 'I know you said cherries, but I felt like doing lilies this time!' – after they've paid me a lot of money. So working with families where the trust is already established means a lot to me, and in those cases I will do whatever I can to help them if the road looks a little rocky. And sometimes it definitely does!

Last spring I got a call about engagement dresses for two sisters. I had known the family for years, made the wedding dresses for their sisters and I'd done lots of Communion dresses and engagement outfits for them too. I was really fond of their mum, having met her years ago at a wedding, and with all the dresses I'd made for her she trusted me too.

The family is from Belfast, where engagement parties are a really big deal and always require a separate, specific outfit. They have long engagements, sometimes from when they're about 14. These two – Patricia and Marie – were a bit older than that and they chose similar engagement dresses but in different colours, as they had got engaged on the same day and wanted to create a bit of a theme. Marie's dress was red, and Patricia's was yellow. Having only met the girls' mum, I worked 'blind' on those two dresses. I was sent measurements and we sent them back designs in the post. At first it's quite a stressful way to work but when you get it right, it's magic!

When the dresses were en route to the girls, I remember their mum calling and asking if I had sent them.

Me and My Big Mouth: Patricia

'Yes, love, they're on their way,' I replied.

'Ooh good, thank you so much!' she said. 'Those girls have been sitting at the windy for days.'

'What, love?' I asked.

'They've been at the windy, love – I think they'd be there forever if I didn't know they had the dresses on the way!'

'That's great, then,' I said, confused.

When the call ended I went into the factory and spoke to the girls.

'Have you ever heard this expression before – "At the windy"? I am so confused!'

'Does it mean they're excited?' asked Leanne.

Some of the others chipped in with their suggestions while we had a cuppa and scratched our heads. Eventually Pauline worked it out. 'They're at the window! They're sitting in the window for the postman!'

Aha! I thought of all the fiancées waiting for their dresses and smiled. Later that night I told my partner Dave about my confusion and we had a little chuckle to ourselves. A day or two later the mum called to say the dresses were perfect and the girls had been thrilled. I was thrilled too, and I was just as delighted when they asked me to do the wedding dresses for later that year.

Marie went for hearts all over hers, and she got married first. The wedding was a great day, a huge success. Patricia was to be married a few months later and that was when things got complicated.

Me and My Big Mouth: Patricia

By the time Patricia came to designing her dress, it was the third big event her family had that year, and her dad had fallen ill and could no longer work. Her mum was frantic and it was a rough time.

They were a great family, though – they had dignity and were really respectful to me. Instead of having tense conversations where they were embarrassed or ashamed, the mum was totally up front with me about the situation at home and all the stress she had. It would not have worked for that wedding to be postponed – it's not a culture where they can just put weddings off. The daughters had got engaged together so it was only right and fair that they got married close together. The wedding is so important for travellers, it signifies so much – and Patricia needed a dress just as special as Marie's.

She had her heart set on a shell theme and sent me a drawing of her dream dress, with hundreds of scalloped shells all overlapping across the bodice, covered in 3D diamanté and fronds of delicate fabric around the waist as floating seaweed. It was gorgeous.

I already knew that things were difficult for Annie by this point, so when I saw the 'dream design', I was determined to make them something really special.

So I had a bit of a chat with Leanne, and we set about thinking creatively to see how we could get the most for this family at a time when they could do with a bit of a boost. There were a few cups of coffee, a few long discussions and a few tweaks here and there before we sent a variety of ideas back to Belfast. What made this process even easier was that by now I had seen pictures of the engagement dresses on the girls, so I had a much better idea of what I was working with.

We knew exactly what would suit Patricia and how to accommodate both her shape and her dream design to get the best possible finished look.

Leanne and I really dug in and I was pretty proud of the concept that we came up with in the end, as we managed to incorporate a lot of sparkle as well as the shell and seaweed detail that Patricia wanted so much – and of course the classic skirts! It was a treat to be able to start work on it.

By the time the dress was nearly made, I was closer than ever to the mum, Annie.

I could have a real laugh with her on the phone – even when she was having such a hard time she always had a smile and a chuckle. No detail was a hassle for her; she'd bared her soul to me and was confident in the love of her family but she still had a lot on. I took her calls whenever she could get back to me because I trusted this family: I knew the situation.

For a while I had suspected that with the dad unwell they might not be able to leave home to come over and collect the dress themselves as is usual, so I had kept an ear to the ground for anyone driving over around that time. I was thrilled when I found someone.

'Listen, love,' I told the mum a few weeks before we finished the dress. 'I know a guy who goes over to Ireland the whole time – I can save you the boat trip. Just give him a pint when you can.'

'Oh, Thelma, would you?' said Annie. 'I was just starting to worry about that. That'd be brilliant, so fantastic of you!'

'Well, you can put it to the back of your mind, and I'll sort it out with him.'

But then disaster struck. About a week before he was due to make the trip, the fella had an accident and was unable to drive over to Belfast. But I didn't have the heart to tell the girls he couldn't do it, I just thought I'd have to find someone else. They couldn't come to me and couriers cost a fortune for my dresses – you need half a dozen different-sized boxes to fit all the bits in – so I felt it was my responsibility. I'd offered them the deal to try and help out, so now I had to make good on it. There was no way I could go back on my word at this point.

The calls began a day later. They'd paid in full, the dress was finished. There was no reason for it not to be on the way.

Me and My Big Mouth: Patricia

'Hiya, Thelma love – do you know what day your fella's coming over?'

'I've not managed to get hold of him yet, but he knows he's not going long so don't you worry!'

I put my phone down and stared at it, wondering at what I'd just said. I simply couldn't bring myself to tell her.

Day two: another call.

'Sorry to bother you, Thelma, love, just checking if you got hold of your fella yet?'

'He left me a message last night, Annie. I'll try and call him back now!'

Day three: a third call.

'Hiya, Thelma.'

'Oh Annie, I forgot! I'll call him right now for you, love.'

Day four: an even bigger lie.

'Hiya, Thelma, love–'

'Hi, this isn't Thelma, it's her daughter.'

'Ooh you do sound alike! Is your mum there? I need to check about a delivery. It's Annie, the Macdonagh wedding.'

'She's out at the moment but I'll let her know you called.'

By this point the girls in the office had cottoned on to what I was doing and they were none too impressed.

'Why are you lying like this?' asked Pauline. 'She's such a lovely woman – she deserves the truth.'

Me and My Big Mouth: Patricia

'I just feel so guilty,' I would try and explain. But the simple fact was I'd got myself into a double bind where I felt bad because I wasn't dealing with the situation but then again I wasn't dealing with the situation because I felt so bad.

'Just tell her,' encouraged Pauline. 'It was a big favour to start with. She'll just have to come and pick it up – they'll find a way.'

'I feel terrible,' I confessed. 'I have no plan B. Or C ... or D.'

Day five: I could tell Annie was starting to suspect something was up.

'I can't get hold of him, love,' I admitted. 'But the dress will be there – don't worry.'

'I won't, love. And I can't thank you enough for sorting this out – I just don't know what I would have done without you!'

I think she thought I was about to tell her that the dog had eaten my homework, and she wasn't far wrong.

I'll find someone, I told myself. But there was no one.

By the Thursday I had done everything and asked everyone. There wasn't a single person I hadn't called for help. The situation was about to get out of control. Annie's trust in me was 100 per cent. She knew that the dress would be with her because I had repeatedly reassured her it would be, and I had broken her trust. To be honest, I felt like shit. Then it dawned on me: I was just going to have to take the dress

Me and My Big Mouth: Patricia

myself. I worked late that night, trying to get as much done for the next day as I possibly could – I didn't want to leave the rest of the team in it on top of everything else.

When I got home Dave was already in bed. It was 2am. I climbed in gently beside him and prodded him a little to wake him.

'Dave. Dave. Dave …'
'Mmm?'
'Do you fancy a trip to Ireland?'
'You what?'
'Dave, do you fancy a trip to Ireland?'

'Sure. When?' I think he was perhaps dreaming of Guinness and some beautiful walks.

'Tomorrow. First thing tomorrow,' I whispered.

He sat bolt upright.

'What?!'

'Listen, I'll tell you the whole story from the beginning on the road but the long and short of it is we need to go to Ireland tomorrow.'

'Save it,' he said. 'I'll listen tomorrow in the van. But one of these days your mouth is going to get you into big trouble – you need to stop making promises that you can't actually deliver. This is madness, whatever you're up to.'

Me and My Big Mouth: Patricia

He was right.

'I know you'd do exactly the same if you were me,' I said. I knew I was right too – it had to be done.

'We'll go tomorrow first thing then,' he said, slumping back into the bed.

'Sleep well, love – see you in the morning!'

I smiled as I drifted off to sleep, finally relaxed, knowing the dress would be there on time.

Luckily Dave is a self-employed builder, so he could take the day off fairly easily once he had been into the office first thing and paid all the lads. Meanwhile, I went into my office and broke the news that I was going to take the dress myself.

'I've found a way to take the dress!' I said to Leanne, standing at the kettle. 'It's this amazing guy who's going to drive it there for me!'

'Oh my God, you're kidding! Who?' she asked.

'What's his name?' said Pauline.

'Dave!' I replied.

'You what?' said Leanne.

'Yeah, we're setting off in a minute,' I told them.

The rest of the office was gobsmacked. They could not believe I'd let a situation get so out of hand that I was now making Dave drive me to Northern Ireland. But there was nothing else for it.

Me and My Big Mouth: Patricia

I decided to take Katrina out of school so she could come with us – I knew we wouldn't be able to get there and back in a day. We got a boat for about 2pm that Friday, from Holyhead to Belfast. The drive from Liverpool to Holyhead is about two hours. Katrina knows what we're like, and she's been chatting to these people's kids for years – she knows I go over for weddings. She was completely unfazed by it all and happy to sit in the back of the car. Meanwhile, in the front seat my phone was going, and going and going. It was physically hot from the constant ringing; it was non-stop. But I could not bring myself to call Annie back until we were actually on the boat because then I would know that there was no way the dress would not get to her.

But then my phone only went and died as we drove into the port, leaving me with no way to get in touch with her at all. I knew this would mean she'd worry that I had cut her off, that there was no dress and it was not coming.

I imagined her running through worse-case scenarios in her head as we drove onto the ferry. It was agony that just as I knew everything was going to be OK, she was reaching a fever pitch. I couldn't even turn my phone on to get her number and call her from Dave's – we were stuck on the boat with no way to make contact. There was only one thing for it: we had to keep going.

The boat trip took about three hours, and they were three very silent hours. We had a meal and a drink but I just kept staring at the sea, wishing the boat would somehow hurry

Me and My Big Mouth: Patricia

up. I wasn't nervous about the dress, I just felt dreadful for Annie. On the one hand I knew it would be a nice surprise to see the family, but I didn't like to think about the worrying they must have been doing then. Dave is very laid-back and just encouraged me to try and think of it as a nice day out of the office.

'I can't stop thinking of that girl at the windy,' I told him. 'She'll be frantic!'

We drove straight from the boat to their house, which took about an hour. A gorgeous spring evening, it was just starting to get lighter in the evenings and there was a really lovely hazy sunlight as we made the drive. It was about to happen, and I began to get excited.

'They're going to die …' I started to say to Dave and Katrina.

'I can't believe you've done this …' Dave was still saying.

'I can't wait to see their faces, Mum!' said Katrina, now hardly able to contain herself in the back seat.

When we got to their street I immediately remembered a lot of travellers lived there, as I'd done other weddings with paperwork addressed to other houses in the same street. I knew it was long, so we turned onto it and slowly drove, trying to see the house numbers. At this point I realised people might recognise us and it only took a couple of minutes before they did.

We started to see them notice the car, and they began to run alongside it up the street. We were in Dave's Range Rover and it was full to bursting with everything for the dress, from the stack of cardboard boxes containing the bodice and accessories to the skirt itself.

All of the netting was billowing out through the entire back of the car, like Princess Diana's skirt when she arrived at St Paul's Cathedral in the famous Glass Coach. There was no mistaking who we were, or what we had with us.

Katrina pressed her face to the 'windy' and stared out at the kids and teenagers running alongside.

'She's going to flip, Mum – this is so exciting!'

'I think she is, love,' I replied, craning my neck to see if we were nearly there.

Dave continued to drive slowly and carefully along the road. Suddenly, a lurch of fear ran through me.

'Oh God,' I said, grabbing Dave's arm. 'They could just kick off at me! They could ask why I put them through this and tell me to leave. Imagine what I'd do if it were Katrina?'

But it was too late to worry any more. Suddenly a surge of people seemed to be coming from everywhere. They were throwing open their front doors and running out to see the commotion – the bush telegraph was well and truly up and

252

running! We saw the house, just as they saw us. Annie and Patricia came running out squealing, jumping up and down.

Everyone swamped around the car, trying to get a look in but I just leapt out and gave Annie and Patricia a huge hug.

'I can't believe it's you!'

'You made it!'

'I'm so sorry I couldn't tell you, my phone died!'

'You're here, you're here!'

All the neighbours were standing around whooping and yelling, people were applauding and shouting congratulations. I have never seen an atmosphere like it – it was obvious this family was as well-liked in their community as they were by me and the team. Everyone was crying – cousins, aunties, the lot. They just kept pouring out of the house, holding each other in shock that the dress was actually there, only a few hours before the big day.

Annie's husband came out of the house and shook Dave's hand, thanking him for everything he had done. They exchanged a look that I'm pretty sure meant: women!

This was the first time I had ever met Patricia in person and she was exactly as her photographs of the engagement party suggested. A smiling, happy creature, she was as chatty as she was charming. She had the most gorgeous Irish accent and was really softly spoken, even though she was shrieking with glee at how everything had turned out. Like a kid in a sweet shop, she was really excited and fluttering with nerves. She couldn't stop crying – her emotions were bubbling over and running everywhere at speed.

Me and My Big Mouth: Patricia

Within an instant she started squealing that she wanted to try the dress on. Understandably, she could scarcely believe that it actually existed.

The living room was about five by five metres, though. Once all the boxes and the skirts were inside, there was not much room at all − especially as it was full of furniture too. Eventually I got the fleet of aunties and cousins to leave so I could help Patricia into it. I couldn't even get it on her while standing in the room so I had to climb on a sofa and lean down. There was a mini-bride too, who had to try hers on in the kitchen.

They met at the doorways and could not believe it. Patricia and her mini-replica turned to face each other and gasped as each realised how lovely the other looked. Their dresses matched crystal for crystal, with all the little seaside details shimmering in the light. Calm now that her dress was there, Patricia looked almost regal compared to her little mini-bride's excitement. It's one of my favourite things about mini-brides − the way they remind you how great the magical bride is looking too. None of us could really get over what had happened at all.

Then, when they were standing there, I finally worked up the courage to say to Annie: 'I'll tell you now, that fella hasn't been coming for the last week. I just didn't know how to tell you − I couldn't get anyone else to do it.'

Annie gasped. 'I knew you wouldn't let us down,' she insisted, 'we always trusted you.'

There were no recriminations at all.

After all the excitement and tears, we squeezed back into the living room and found a spot for everyone to sit down and enjoy a cup of tea. The family begged us to stay for the wedding, but we had thrown such a random selection of things into our bags, we really weren't ready for the occasion at all.

It was wonderful to spend time with them that evening, though, after everything we'd been through together.

When I look back on that wedding now, I don't remember the dress, even though they sent me some gorgeous photos the next day. This time, all I remember is the people. It's been a real privilege to get so close to families in times of high emotion, and earning their trust means a lot to me. Working with this family was very special. Patricia made a gorgeous bride, and I'm sure she's a wonderful wife too!

It has been amazing to be part of weddings like Patricia's, and an adventure to be part of some of the more challenging girls' weddings, too. When my own marriage ended, I could never have dreamed that weddings would become such a huge part of my life again – and I wouldn't have it any other way!

Me and My Big Mouth: Patricia

Acknowledgements

Firstly I'd like to say a massive thank you to all my fantastic Nico staff − we've been on quite a journey together over the past couple of years and I couldn't have done it without each and every one of you.

Thank you to everybody at Firecracker Films and Channel 4 for your continued support.

Thank you to Alex Heminsley for your editing of the text. And thank you to the team at HarperCollins.

I'd also like to thank all of the travellers I have worked with. There have been some interesting moments along the way, and it hasn't always been easy, but I will forever be grateful that you let me into your world and gave me the chance to understand your wonderful culture. I have made some amazing friends over the years.